CONNECTIONS

Bishop Lyttelton
Library
Winchester

'Only connect! That was the whole of the sermon.'
E. M. Forster, *Howards End*

In memory of Celia my sister
and for James who told me
to write this book

J. L. HOULDEN

CONNECTIONS

The Integration of Theology and Faith

SCM PRESS LTD

British Library Cataloguing in Publication Data

Houlden, J. L.
  Connections: the integration of theology
  and faith.
  1. Theology
  I. Title
  230   BR118

  ISBN 0–334–00263–X

First published 1986
by SCM Press Ltd,
26–30 Tottenham Road, London N1

Photoset at The Spartan Press Ltd
Lymington, Hants
Printed in Great Britain by
Richard Clay (The Chaucer Press) Ltd
Bungay, Suffolk

CONTENTS

v

PREFACE

This book is a whole presented in two parts. Part One consists of a self-contained sequence of argument and reflection. Its aim is to describe and alleviate a state of affairs set out in the Introduction. It is about the experience of studying theology and relating it to religious commitment. General discussion prompts questions about the application of principles to particular aspects of belief and practice: how does your theory work in this matter or that? So Part Two consists of a series of essays designed to answer this request. Each stands by itself, but all illustrate the same principles, those that emerge from the discussion in Part One. The effect of the whole is to portray a certain attitude at work.

The book tries to meet a situation which is often referred to but from which people shy away. It gets far too little sustained treatment. Some have given up hope of making coherent sense of Christian adherence in the light of scholarship, reconciling the study with the pulpit or the pew. Some are even satisfied that each should work on its own independent lines. Then the way is open to being content with the strident orthodoxies and unyielding postures without which church life often seems incapable of operating, so reflecting corresponding trends in other areas of life. There are those, however, who go on entertaining the claims of careful truthfulness in the setting of religious commitment, despite much discouragement. They keep hoping to see how it 'all fits together'. The idea of what follows is to strengthen their arm, just as it arises from their much too silent witness. Their manifest need has enabled the book to be written.

Once upon a time, theology was the articulation of man's quest for God and man's reponse to him. This book is in effect a return to that perspective, but (such is its hope) without compromising that sense of integrity which modern theological study has taught us to prize above rubies.

Like any teacher, I owe thanks to my pupils and to others with whom these ideas have been discussed; also to friends without whose happy interruptions the work of writing might have grown tedious. I owe particular thanks to John Drury, Stuart Hall and Nicholas Henshaw for thoughts; to John Bowden for waiting and encouraging; and to Shelagh Brown for typing the manuscript.

PART ONE

-1-

Introduction

This book is written for those who have in common the experience of studying theology. Or rather, it is written for some of them. It is written for those who, whether in the midst of it or afterwards, find the experience invigorating but also problematic and a source of unease, because of lack of unity whether in the study itself or in its relationship with religious commitment and the religious quest.

It is not written for those who cheerfully receive what their teachers give, find it sufficiently satisfactory, leap the statutory hurdles placed before them, and then rest content. Nor is it for those who study theology with their minds already formed on what is to be believed by the faithful Christian, absorb from their study what fortifies that belief, decline what challenges it, and so emerge unaltered and serene. Nor again is it for those (a growing group) who study theology as unconnected with religious belief, that is without a close personal interest in the profound issues of human life in relation to God to which the study directs them.

So this book is for those who both open themselves to the experience and find it puzzling and perhaps alarmingly incomplete. That does not mean that they are deterred or deflated by it. It means that they are concerned with questions of overall coherence, with connections between the different parts of their study, and with a hope that the study will not only train the mind in some general way but also strengthen life and

3

deepen understanding in the matter of God. Everything in this book presupposes experience of this kind and comments on it from one angle or another. Those who are not in the intended audience are likely to find much of it unnecessary, over-scrupulous or perverse.

It is worth conducting an exploration of this area because, among those who share the reaction just described, there is much bewilderment. They do not form a party or an identi-fiable school; often they do not know where to turn for comfort and light. They are quite commonly subject to misunderstand-ing, scorn and even hostility at the hands of those whose study of theology has not produced this reaction as well as religious people who have not studied. They are open to charges of tampering with true religion and weakening faith, and no course is clearly charted for them to follow. They move in unknown waters. Nobody gives much help with the task of enabling theological study to yield a consistent and united outlook. Zig-zag movements of mind, hand-to-mouth exped-ients, shafts of illumination breaking into a featureless cloudy sky – these are often the best that can be hoped for, as the mind matures in response to education and experience.

Perhaps there is no reason why theological study should now lead to a united outlook, and it is a hope which it is futile to entertain. As we shall see in the next chapter, theological study presents itself as a variable collection of distinct subjects, and their co-existence in a curriculum or a faculty can appear merely a matter of convention or convenience. Nowadays its make-up may depend on factors as fortuitous as the interests of a particular group of teachers. Each subject has its own modes of operation, highly developed among its practitioners, little known outside. Each makes its own demands and offers its own rewards. Theological study means, in practice, exposure to a certain number of them, a set of independent experiences, each self-sufficient, existing in its own right and asserting its own expertise. Together, inevitably and by mysterious chemistry, they work certain effects in the minds of those who study. But these are not planned or deliberately engineered or even so much as suggested by those who provide the means of study. Now, only the narrowest and most secluded kind of institution offers to bring about a conscious, comprehensive and overt theological understanding, and it earns mistrust and obloquy for its pains.

Where such effects are not planned by those who teach, their occurrence is unbidden. They steal upon the student and often their presence is only realized long after their arrival. Thus, any total effect of theological study is unintended and unprovided for – a by-product of study, something of an accident. It is, in formal terms, unreflective, or rather it comes to the level of reflection piecemeal, incoherently, and with infinite diversity among individuals. All the weight of intellectual discipline rests with the particular subjects, hardly any with the total human result. Implicit in the study is the duty to be exercised and informed in the subjects. That is the public requirement and expectation. What may follow is a bonus, wholly optional, no business of academic authorities, and not a matter of considered intellectual discipline. Everything conspires to make it amateur, haphazard, private and uncertain in scope and development. No wonder many refuse to let such effects of study arise within them and, for total outlook, fall back on simple, given patterns of belief which study is not permitted to affect. Ultimately dangerous, it is at least a recipe for coherent survival of a kind.

This disparateness of level and quality of attention between the content of study and the effect of study is not without commendable aspects. It can claim to free theological study from that taint of indoctrination which has so often been its bane. The less the overall effects are prescribed and the less interest is taken in them by those in control, the freer are those who study to decide for themselves and to go their own ways. The whole business is made more open and flexible, able to be responsive to changing and varied needs. The price paid is that those who study may be insufficiently equipped to go anywhere

5

worth going to. Not only will they avoid being pressed into some orthodox mould; they may fail to get into any particular shape at all.

There are intelligible reasons why the process of theological study seems not to 'add up', why the parts impress much more than the whole; and some of them are good as well as intelligible. A field has to be divided into manageable lots. Theology, like other subjects, has its traditions of organization which have been immensely productive of learning and wisdom, even though the resulting specialization limits what any one person can hope to achieve and divides mind from mind. Such reasons are sufficient to allay possible unease in many who study; for some, indeed, the idea that their studies should 'add up' never arises. Yet for others the hope is never far from the surface. During the actual process of formal study itself, with its many technical and specialized demands, it may for a time be suppressed; but, perhaps more than in any other area of study, pressure towards 'adding up' is likely to be prominent among the motives which prompted the choice of the subject in the first place and to figure in subsequent reflection on what has been achieved. In many cases, vocational demands will bring it to the fore: those who have studied theology will often find themselves expected to possess not just expert knowledge of the Bible or the church's history, the fruit of distinct disciplines, but a coherent mind on the profoundest questions of human destiny. A legitimate anxiety about unmerited suffering is not sated (though it may be illicitly relieved) by a recital of the Bible's or the Christian tradition's various views on the subject: what is required is something that the one consulted has made his own, in relation to a total understanding and indeed to an intelligible stance in life. Even where vocational responsibility is not a factor, the inner heart makes its own insistent demands. A student of theology (as of any other subject) is not just a student. 'Being human' carries with it at any rate a latent pressure towards reflection on the great matters which are the central concerns of theology and of religion, and a study of theology may rightly be expected to lead in due course to greater maturity of thought and more articulate discourse about them.

A discouraging cloud hovers over this wholly understandable felt need to achieve a coherent outlook as a fruit of theological study and not just a body of disparate information or even a degree of mastery of a number of intellectual disciplines. There must be the suspicion that it simply cannot be achieved any longer. It may once have been within theology's scope, but is so no more. The demands of the human heart and of certain vocational roles (of priest or teacher) simply cannot be met. In response to pressure for intelligible help in the face of unmerited suffering, all that anyone may be capable of delivering, other than untrained wisdom, is fragments of information, a retailing of what texts and tradition may say. These may indeed not just inform but also edify, stimulate and so comfort the anxious questioner, but they do not go as far as a rationale, a way of dealing with the whole matter. It is true that a training in philosophy of religion or the work of systematic theologians may yield more than mere information from scripture and history, and will work towards the end in view, but in practice they often seem out of tune with those more historical disciplines – to the student's confusion. It may still seem that to ask for a coherent outlook is to cry for the moon. Once visible and in a way accessible, it is now eclipsed. For many centuries, Christian theology was indeed a unified business:[1] those aspects of concern which we distinguish as doctrine, ethics and spirituality (how to think, live and pray) were commonly felt as a single whole. The quest for God, in terms of understanding and holiness, was a single pursuit. Of course, looking back on the Christian literature of past times, we can now distinguish these aspects of thought within it, and it is an analytical convenience to do so; but that is anachronistic, as far as the perception of the past writers is concerned. To go back right to the start, we may write books on 'the ethics of the Gospel of Matthew', isolating the writer's treatment of what we now call ethical questions, but he was aware of no such agenda. He never said to himself, 'I must now consider how to present Jesus' ethical teaching and how Christians should solve a range of ethical problems': he wrote a unified account, to an agenda formed on other grounds. So there is a certain falsity in forcing our distinctions on those who wrote before ever they came into awareness. At the same time, they only heighten our sense of the difficulty in achieving a comparable unity for ourselves.

Another kind of falsity emerges if we try to recover for our own use exactly the unified theological awareness which they possessed; for there is, once more, anachronism in making transfers of past achievements to an alien present, as if old ways could live again. But even though it is hopeless to try to reanimate some unified outlook from the past, it is not hopeless to seek unity of theological outlook in any form. The past may indeed serve to instruct us how it may *not* now be open to us. It may warn us off the inclination to go down certain obsolete roads, but it does not close all possible roads. For the pressure towards unity of outlook is strong. It is natural and praise-worthy to want to be all of a piece, even though our under-standing may in fact only gradually or fitfully be extended over the areas which are to be unified.

The forming of such an integrated theological outlook is, indeed, a never-finished exercise. New areas of knowledge, new kinds of experience continually enter the process for each of us. Its very essence is resolute inclusiveness. It is anathema to the interest before us in this book to say of any relevant matter: 'On this subject my mind is finally made up and I shall not allow evidence or experience to alter my belief.' So the pressure towards unity of mind is necessarily accompanied by a sense that its achievement is always provisional.

Without doubt the way is largely uncharted, and the terms on which, for us, a unified theological outlook is possible are uncertain and often uncongenial. For one thing, it seems that one person's way of integration must be different from another's. Over long periods of Christian history, the rightness

8

of not only interior unity but also outward uniformity of theological outlook in the context of religious commitment seemed so plain that it is still hard for many to think otherwise without a feeling of abnormality or even guilt. For another thing, it seems probable that different possible frameworks of integration need formal exploration, so that the whole matter is more in the open, more available for discussion. The frameworks may relate to 'states of life' (teacher, priest, black, single, professional person, politician) or to intellectual bases of operation or to casts of mind (a starting-point in the study of the New Testament or the thought of a classical theologian or a style of prayer or a burning social concern).

Of the persons for whom this book is written, there is not one who does not already make some pretence to the integrated outlook that is in mind. To feel the necessity of it is to begin to obtain it, with whatever naivety or inadequacy. They will understand the inevitability of the diversity which is entailed and may even see it as something to be welcomed. But it has to be admitted that, as things stand, it often leads to frustration. Many experts in one of the branches of theology, whose life may involve inhabiting a narrow area of study, go beyond its frontiers and have arrived at what they would see as 'total theology', especially if they are pressed by religious commitment to do so. It is ironic, however, how rarely it carries conviction with others equally skilled, whether in their own field or, especially, in other fields of enquiry. It is a commonplace that theologians of different backgrounds fail to understand one another, let alone see eye to eye. Indeed, the nonspecialist student of theology may be, in this respect, at an advantage, for he or she may have a balance of interest which the specialist has forfeited.

It is a question of some interest whether this is just a fact of our situation, to be endured when it cannot be enjoyed, or a state of affairs capable of improvement. There is little doubt that it derives in part from the fact that so little attention has been paid for many years to the business of integration that we lack a tradition of skill in the matter. Without that skill, a creative approach to diversity of approach has not been developed, and the adumbrations of unity which people experience lack coherence and direction. The relationships between the accustomed theological disciplines and the conditions on which a unified outlook is obtainable are so little considered, and the interests which make for maintaining the compartments of study intact are so strong, that there simply must be room for improvement, and, given the will, there could be movement. At present, everything makes for a situation where the level of theological coherence drops as a person crosses the frontier out of his sphere of expertise or from one field of study to another; that is, as he moves towards the formation of that unified theological outlook without which humanity seems deficient and the intelligent practical application of theological study unlikely. We shall see that there are some reasons to hope[2] that the manifest need to improve the situation is prompting the discussion that alone can give rise to the discovery of remedies.

In the following chapters, there is first an account of two sources of our present discontent – the fragmentation of theology as a single and coherent study, and the alienation of theology from religion. Then there is an examination of steps towards greater integration. Part Two of the book contains a number of 'set pieces' – in effect, essays on topics germane to our concern and written with the attitudes of Part One in mind. They serve as examples of the possibilities available to those who choose this path.

-2-

The Disintegration of Theology

The content of theological study is not something which prescribes itself. It is capable of development, it has been subject to change, and it is susceptible of further change. At the moment, it is strong on expertness in its various parts, weak on rationale as a whole. This weakness is often admitted, yet rarely attended to. In its present form and degree, it is a recent development, and for a long time it was scarcely realized.

There is no need here even to outline the story of what the study of Christian theology has, over its long history, been understood to be.[1] It is enough to say that until the last two centuries, its purpose was overtly and plainly religious, however academic the means used for its achievement. That is to say, its aim was the development of man's capacity to relate to God and the articulation of that relationship in human words and concepts. In that sense, though it distinguished different intellectual pursuits (the exegesis of scripture, the elucidation of doctrines within a philosophical framework), it was overwhelmingly a unified study, held together by concerns which are now commonly assigned to the realm of spirituality, that is, to a specialist (and often marginal) area within theological study. In its effects on theological study, the Enlightenment brought both a new intellectual independence and a secularized quest for truth, both historical and conceptual, in its own right. It led naturally to specialization and to the self-sufficient assurance of discrete fields of study (scripture, doctrine, church

11

history, ethics). They were kept together by a common ancestry in the old, much more unified, theological pursuit of earlier times and, vitally, by their common role in what was seen as the necessary equipment of the clergy, for whose training the theological enterprise at that time almost exclusively existed. But as intellectual disciplines they drew apart, developed in increasing isolation from each other, and derived their self-assurance, their standing in the world, from their participation in the increasingly secular aspirations of the universities where they had their chief homes.

Sometimes the secularization and the drawing apart were disguised and hardly apparent even to those living in the midst of the process. For instance, in those English universities where the Anglican tradition was dominant, both the appearance of theology as a unified discipline and the conveying of what looked like an integrated theological outlook, all in a context of Christian commitment, survived until recent times. The influential Anglican appeal to the Bible and the Fathers meant that a syllabus which concentrated on the study of the Old and New Testaments and the history of doctrinal development in the first five centuries of the Christian era, looked like an education in theology as a coherent and unified discipline in the old style – even though the subjects were taught in a modern critical way.[2] And the impression was fortified when a single tutor guided his pupils through all subjects (a practice still found in Oxford twenty years ago), counting specialist competence of less account than the opportunity for encounter with a supposedly coherent theological mind, which might reckon to see the whole field in some kind of unity. The proximity of worship in a college chapel completed the picture. It was one of the last models to preserve the appearance (but how critically?) and, perhaps, in limited ways, the reality of theology as a unified study, with consistent intellectual and religious aims.

Nevertheless, the twin processes of secularization and the drawing apart of subjects dominated the scene. In sheer quantitative terms, though conceptual study played a part (that is, questions of the truth and comprehension of theological ideas), the weight of attention fell more and more on history. Whether it was the Bible or Christian doctrine, the essence of study was enquiry into the history which related to the matter in hand. The emphasis shifted from the needs of the present, seen as provided for in authoritative texts, to the texts themselves, seen as phenomena of the past which possessed continuing authority and interest. The proportions of these two qualities, authority and interest, was a matter of adjustable balance, and the sense in which the former might legitimately persist became ever more difficult to define; but both had long been present and it depended on circumstances which predominated and how the authority of the past was to be understood, in a world whose differences from the past became ever more apparent. As we saw, the growth of emphasis on the historical, studied in a number of distinct academic subjects, did not immediately lead to the loss of the sense of theological study as a unified pursuit, especially if that study were sponsored and blessed by ecclesiastical authorities. Where, as in England, ecclesiastical influence remained strong (in creating an aura, at least), it often had a restraining effect on scholarship,[3] not in the sense of producing dishonest conformity with traditional orthodoxy in people who knew it to be false, but in creating an atmosphere of sobriety in which the more radical options in the understanding of historical questions, such as the life of Jesus, tended to be avoided. There was a tendency to go for solutions of a more traditional kind to problems like the truth of Jesus' resurrection, and there was consternation and disturbance when vistas opened up which rendered the theologically authoritative role of the programme of accredited study precarious, as for example at the time of R. H. Lightfoot's Bampton Lectures.[4] Then, the balance moved from authority to scholarly interest, and it was hard to take – even for Lightfoot himself.

Yet it is puzzling that there was such consternation, for all along the historical approach had carried in itself the threat of uselessness, when it came to the attainment of a unified theological outlook in present circumstances. It was as if this body of knowledge which one should acquire, concerning these traditional repositories of Christian orthodoxy and authority, was not really meant for lively use in a present theological context, had no existential purpose, but existed in its own right as a reassuring and impressive body of learning. It was to be acquired chiefly by the clergy, as a culture which was enriching and strengthening, and to be experienced as a vehicle of authority which resided in itself and apart from its particular contents – after the manner of an icon whose power depends on response to it for its own sake and by no means on analysis of its construction or artistic properties. It is true that bits of those contents might be spread more widely, as other people might be interested to share this historical knowledge which was chiefly the clergy's preserve. The possession of such knowledge gives a kind of power as one gains familiarity with one's heritage. But when it came to the expression of theological judgment in the present, those provided with such learning found themselves ill-equipped: it was not always satisfactory simply to rehearse the texts and tenets of the past. So it has seemed inevitable to many to fall back on more personal reflection, largely unaided by theological study, on homespun wisdom or 'sanctified common sense'. People could easily sink into incoherence, for the authoritative body of theological teaching, now so largely purveyed historically, failed to yield a unified theological outlook, but only a range of historical information. Knowledge of the Synoptic Problem or the formation of the Nicene Creed stood on one side of a gulf; on the other side were everyday theological questions like the prevalence of suffering in human life or the application of Christian judgment in the political sphere. On the one side academic rigour prevailed, on the other a brand of Christian judgment to which the dominant academic disciplines failed to contribute in any direct way. When it came to the significance of Jesus, it was all too easy to reduce to silence those informed only about the New Testament terms or the patristic categories of thought used to describe it –

as Stevie Smith devastatingly showed.[5] All this is now so obviously disturbing that it takes an effort to see how, so recently, it could seem otherwise, being taken for granted, and how the disintegration of theology as a unified pursuit, firmly in progress for more than two centuries, could in some situations at least be so long delayed in coming to full actuality and, even more, in meeting recognition.

We have seen that a tradition of authority long held the Old Testament, the New Testament and patristic theology together, at least in Anglican circles, when, from the religiously neutral viewpoint of the scholarly world, they, like other subjects, became increasingly distinct from each other and were going their own independent ways as professional pursuits. Links between them, such as there were, came to be based on academic, not theological, considerations. With the decline of that tradition of authority, it has become conventional to find the bond between the distinct disciplines in the idea of *the Christian tradition*. A programme of theological study is seen as concerned with that tradition, and its existence as justified because this concern is common to its various components. The tradition is so long and rich that in practice any actual course of study is bound to be selective, and questions may arise – and receive different answers in different quarters – about what is central and what is peripheral. But there is agreement on the nature of the enterprise – the study of the Christian tradition – and indeed about central aspects of it, above all the Bible and the central corpus of Christian belief, without which that study would be radically defective.

This general description can, however, be too ready an answer to the question of unity, too tempting a way of evading difficulty. As far as it goes, it is of course accurate, just as it accurately describes the natural sciences to say that they are all concerned with the phenomena of nature. But it does nothing to meet the difficulties that arise from the widely differing conventions and methods of the academic disciplines which are included in theological study. It serves only to conceal the degree to which the findings of one subject are only with difficulty assimilated by another, to whose interests they may in fact be highly relevant; and it does nothing to address the question with which this book is concerned: the formation of a unified theological outlook in a context of religious commitment or quest.

Academic subjects exist in the minds and the books of those who have devoted themselves to them and are expert in them. They also form the experience of those who, as students, are exposed, not just to one of them but to a group. It is their position which particularly displays the weaknesses of remaining content with 'the Christian tradition' as a sufficiently unifying, bond-making description of theological study. Think of the neophyte making his way through such a programme as this: the history, religion and literature of Israel, witnessed in the Old Testament and in its Near Eastern context; the historical and literary origins of Christianity, with their numerous intractable problems; the development of Christian belief in the setting of Greek culture and the Roman Empire; the present systematic articulation of the body of Christian beliefs accepted in the church, in the light of fundamental philosophical considerations and of the contemporary culture; the history of the church in the world of the sixteenth century. It makes a course fascinating in the variety of its content and challenging in the range of intellectual skills required. But it betokens a study which is all pieces and no obvious whole, a wheel of spokes and no hub. It leaves all the connections and all the work of forming a unified theological outlook to the individual who experiences it. As we have already seen, it is the disparateness between the effort and sophistication involved in the separate subjects and the indifference and chanciness which attend the work of synthesizing that is both staggering and disturbing.

It may be objected that the connecting and the unifying is not the business of the academic process itself. It is the business of those whose interests are bound up with integrated theological outlooks, such as churches with a message to proclaim. They, presumably, have a special concern with overall coherence and with theological synthesis. They are guardians of a tradition of belief and teaching which it is their task to hand on in intelligible form to subsequent generations. Churches may in fact welcome this responsibility as wholly appropriate.

But quite apart from questions of the adequacy of the resources of churches to mount such operations at a decent level of competence, there are misconceptions in such a proposal. In so far as they are to speak convincingly within their wider cultural setting and in such a way as to take account of the intellectual agenda of the society around them, churches cannot operate in isolation from their environment. Though, as we shall see, churches may have their own angle on the task of synthesis,[6] they have no intellectual reserves all their own, ideas and evidence that are privy to themselves and unknown to those engaged in theological study in secular settings, no special techniques for reaching the truth on controverted questions. There are no theological rabbits lurking in ecclesiastical hats. Much theological study, especially in its intense sharpening of historical awareness, has had the effect of taking the student 'behind the scenes', revealing how theology *works*: that is, showing that hallowed beliefs and sacrosanct concepts are not the deliverances of sheer authority, as if timeless in character, but derive from precise, identifiable and describable settings, from which we have learnt to distance ourselves, holding them as we examine them, as it were in the palm of our hands. This effect of modern theological study constitutes a kind of loss of innocence, with all its customary pains as well as the growth in maturity of which it is the necessary condition. The situation is as much a matter of fact for those in churches as it is for those in university departments, even if the two groups approach it professionally with different responsibilities in mind. The only escape is that of the ostrich. Churches are then in no position, intellectually or practically, to adopt in isolation what could now only seem arbitrary or doctrinaire measures to bring about the kind of synthesis suggested, based on their supposed role as guardians of the tradition of belief. Such styles of unified theological outlook may of course be imposed in the interests of ecclesiastical discipline (e.g. to reduce institutional conflict), but they cannot be seen to grow with integrity out of theological study itself.[7]

There is also the converse point that theological study which is set in the secular sphere is ill-advised to wash its hands of the unifying task: for the academic reason that it offers the possibility of a stimulating new direction of work; for the pastoral and educational reason that a course of study which is all parts and no whole is unbalanced and unfinished; and for the prudential reason that the world at large, to whom academic policy has more and more to justify itself, may see less and less point in the pursuit of specialized studies which have lost a sense of central points of reference and for which the single term 'theology' is a handy cover rather than a realistic description of a field of study.

The subjects which make up theological study have all come to be pulled in two directions: towards theology as a (once) unified pursuit and towards secular disciplines, to whose methods and interests they are closely related. The relative strength of the two pulls varies from scholar to scholar, and indeed from subject to subject. The movement of the subjects into increasingly strong, non-theological fields of academic force is among the main reasons for the fragmentation of theology itself. Thus, it is not surprising that church history as an academic pursuit chiefly presents itself as a branch of history. Vital though it is for anybody seeking a unified theological outlook, if he or she is to avoid false and foolish perspectives and crude abstraction, its subject matter and methods are inextricably linked with those of history in general. Scarcely ever does it now offer a view of the past conditioned by special doctrinal perspectives, and when it does it can hope for no credit.

Doctrinal study, too, has its outside links, without which its work can scarcely find a way to proceed: with history, especially the history of ideas; with philosophy; or with the literary techniques involved in the study of texts. Nevertheless, it leans more strongly than church history towards theology as a unified pursuit, and owes its standing to the recognition of theology as a credible enterprise. It cannot, however, as understood at present, of itself bring about a unified theological outlook. Just because it has developed into a distinct discipline of study, demarcated from other areas, such as biblical studies, even though its concerns demand close relations with them, it cannot claim a right to exclusive leadership in the task of synthesizing. In terms of its broad agenda, and of its affinities with the long tradition of theology as essentially abstract argument and formulation, such a claim looks reasonable, but academic fragmentation has taken its toll here, in what a superficial view may see as the heartland of theology, as elsewhere. Moreover, who can tell how doctrinal study will fare if, as surely it must, it forms more substantial links with other, secular disciplines, such as sociology and psychology, not to speak of close neighbours like biblical study itself?

The case with biblical studies is not dissimilar. Here, too, there are links with the techniques, though not always the ethos or results, of branches of secular study, notably in the textual, literary, historical and hermeneutical areas. But the content, once more, leans towards theology as an overall concern, even though, despite optimistic and persistent attempts, the subject cannot of itself yield a satisfactory unified theology.[8]

A major result of the disappearance of a visible and lively centre in theological study is that the distinct subjects which thrive under its name have not only gone their separate ways but positively run counter to each other in their procedures and achievements. While church historians emphasize that the thought and life of a particular setting must be studied and understood as a totality, distinct from other such totalities of other times and places, liturgical scholars isolate liturgy from such totalities and present the words and ceremonies of Christian worship within a more or less distinct liturgical tradition, viewed diachronically and separated from other aspects of life in the various settings in which liturgy has been formed and used. While New Testament scholars assess and understand the words of Paul in Romans within the immediate context of writing, doctrinal writers are still inclined to ignore such understanding and, without providing notice of any hermeneutical process, to press his words into senses and roles quite other than those of their original setting. Systematic theology is found working with ideas such as 'the resurrection' or 'the Trinity', seemingly oblivious of the historical clarification which they demand and which is available from other disciplines.

In broad terms, inconsistencies and conflicts arise between synchronic modes of perception, where a slice of Christian life and thought is perceived as far as possible in its own right, apart from any necessary expectation of usefulness in later periods including the present, and diachronic modes, where the dominant reality in view is the Christian tradition, more or less isolated as a body of thought or a sphere of life within history and society as a whole and capable of useful examination apart from them. There may be ways of alleviating and even reconciling these two perspectives. Those ways are rarely pursued. Conflict remains, and those who study are left to form their own makeshift accommodations if they are keen to arrive at some kind of intellectual integrity.

-3-

The Alienation of Theology from Religion

There is ample evidence that many people of religious disposition who experience theological study in one form or another find a lack of harmony between the two aspects of themselves involved here. That statement needs a little elucidation. 'Religious disposition' refers here to an underlying or pervasive concern with the quest for God and with openness to God, however that may be conceived. 'Lack of harmony' does not necessarily mean anything as strong as conflict. We have already noticed a number of factors making for such conflict, but harmony can be at risk even where those factors do not arise. Nor is it necessarily a question of naked inconsistency of approach or content, as when, for example, a person sets great religious store by the risen and exalted Jesus but is also aware of acute difficulties in the historical and conceptual understanding of what may be involved. What presents itself is rather a sense of unease at seeming not to be all of a piece, of being subject to disparate pressures. At root, however, it is a matter of deep differences of sensibility between the two modes of perception. They often co-exist, perhaps surprisingly, without too much overt difficulty: people do not always struggle very hard for their own integration and disharmony may even be a source of stimulus. Often people do not perceive that in different aspects of themselves they are travelling on quite distinct tracks, even in contrary directions. The situation may indeed make for their amiability and attractiveness. Yet these differences of sensibility are worth examining both for their own sake and because there may be even greater good to be found in movement towards harmony. After all, deeply divergent though the religious and theological approaches to experience have become in much European culture in the past two or three centuries, they still find points of meeting in many human lives and shared activities. Their co-existence, often inevitable, can easily involve the unhealthy or frustrating pursuit of inconsistent objectives or the acting out of incoherent life-styles. It is not hard to think of instances where the effect is a palpable abdication of common integrity: where individuals and churches use theological apparatus as a smokescreen behind which to further ends that are religious in motivation, employing arguments that the detached observer sees as plainly specious, when the frank avowal of religious concern would be more conducive to the good of all.

Perhaps the most fundamental difference of sensibility between theological study and religion lies in the objectivity required by the former and the personal commitment inseparable from the latter. How can a person be both bound up with and detached from the same object? How can he love it to the depth of his being, yet examine it as if it were under his control and appropriate for his scrutiny? The two moods or (as in a matter of total import such as the question of God and what flows from it) the two ways of life seem utterly inimical to each other. To sit on the fence and to fight in the field on one side of it are actions incapable of simultaneous performance. Yet, before we try to see whether this is the right way to assess the situation, it is worth noting that there are areas of life where we do not find too much difficulty in combining these two attitudes. Not everyone who expresses commitment to a political party to the point of voting for it is devoted to it heart and soul and uncritical of its leaders and policies. Not every collector for a charity is unquestioning of its aims and activities. Not every devoted husband or wife is unaware of the partner's faults and weaknesses. It is true that religious commitment is deeper and wider than these partly analogous loyalties, and by its very nature recoils from what looks like compromise; but, for the moment, we recognize that the psychological feat is far from impossible. Commitment is compatible with certain sorts of detachment. It remains to suggest ways in which this may be intellectually reasonable, and perhaps even religiously desirable. But first, this difference of sensibility merits more examination.

It is often found in a sharper and more involuted form than we have so far recognized, one which relates to a widely felt effect of modern education (in some disciplines obligatory), and which is sometimes both baffling and painful to those who experience it. In it, study and intellectual commitment themselves intertwine. We have to contrast between religious commitment as a matter of heart and will and an intellectual posture which combines the holding of beliefs and opinions with the capacity to observe oneself holding them. The objectivity moves from study into the centre of believing itself. There is built into the business of believing a continuous process of assessment, criticism and development. To believe and yet to be detached from what is believed: these two attitudes come to co-exist. We feel ourselves to be simultaneously both insiders and outsiders. It is a matter of self-criticism not as an occasional virtuous activity but as an essential component of intellectual conviction, and seen now as part of the equipment of a person who is both religiously committed and theologically trained. This distancing of the self from the self, in a posture of simultaneous conviction and self-observation, is highly perplexing to those who have never known it and often feels as if it calls sincerity in question. Of all the problems attended to in this book, this seems the strangest, least clearly entailed by full engagement in theological study. It seems to be a gratuitously self-inflicted torture. But, for good or ill, once it enters a person's system, it establishes itself, and life never feels the same again. I said it was sometimes baffling and painful. The question is whether it is then something simply to be endured, a diseased segment of consciousness which nags even if it does not cripple, but which certainly cannot be regarded positively. At first sight that conclusion seems unavoidable. Even if other tensions and conflicts between commitment and the effects of theological study are resolved, this one, which may seem peculiarly intractable and, with an insidious kind of complexity, to be continually gnawing at the vitals of faith, surely cannot be acquiesced in without a perpetual threat to integrity. It is essentially concerned with a division in the believing self. But such a negative judgment must be unsatisfactory. Far though this kind of detachment seems to be from most traditional attitudes associated with religious commitment (zeal, devotion, single-mindedness), it is important to hold it in a place where it is capable of a creative role in the formation of a unified theological outlook. We shall see in due course ways in which this may be done. Suffice it to say that the element of provisionality, of which it is one manifestation, will impress itself upon us again and again as something currently unfashionable among religious people but both deep in the spirit of the religious quest and thrown up constantly by modern theological study.

The experience just described is often linked with another, which can equally be a source of distress and can help to bring about a situation where a person is pressed into keeping study and commitment in distinct compartments, or else abandoning the one or the other in the interests of maintaining a viable way of life – often at the expense of deeper integrity. The most commonly experienced effect of modern theological study is a sharpening of historical awareness and sensitivity. It is now not just a question of knowing what happened or what it was like to live in some past period (in ancient Israel, in the beginnings of Christianity, or at some stage in the history of the church): for older generations of theological enquirers that was the limit of curiosity and attainment. It is also, for many, an acute

24

realization of how different those former times were both from each other and from our own time. The effect is to bring discontinuities to the fore. What is involved here is not the giving of free rein to cultural relativism, with its attendant difficulties[1] and its only partial correspondence to the facts – not dogmatic attachment to a theory of historical change. Nor is it a matter of ignoring continuities. It is a matter of recognizing that continuities (for example, in institutions or in the verbal forms of religious affirmation) mask deeper and more far-reaching differences of consciousness between one period or place and another than was formerly realized. A heightened imaginative grasp of discrete historical situations is simply a common fact of present intellectual sensibility.[2] Equally, religious commitment is deeply wedded to emphasis on continuity. As a faith and as an institution, the Christian religion, like many others, finds relationship with past and future indispensable to its existence. It depends on awareness of its continuous life through time. Here, then, is a source of tension of whose effects we have scarcely begun to take account.

There is a question whether the particular forms of attachment to continuity characteristic of modern religious commitment are essential to the reality and stability of that commitment or the transient results of relatively recent influences. For example, much of the feeling for continuity found among religious people in Western society is surely a long-term effect of early nineteenth-century romanticism, joined to fear of the loss of landmarks. But at a deeper level, many Christian beliefs are of their very nature closely bound up with a strong insistence on continuity, most notably doctrines concerning the church's ministry. At least in their traditional form, such doctrines seem not to be able to survive a major shift of historical awareness to the side of discontinuity. If what is most strongly in mind when it comes to a consideration of the episcopal or papal office is no longer mere succession in office and title, or continuity in the exercise of certain functions by divine authority, but rather the diverse and changing roles of the officers concerned through the ages, then, where this matter is important to religious commitment, that commitment is bound to be affected.

It is, however, not only a matter of areas where continuity is obviously part of the religious conviction itself. Awareness of whole and discrete historical situations, and so of discontinuity, rubs uncomfortably against even academic enquiry, where it is less historical in emphasis and may seem closer to the ethos of religious commitment. Thus, the task of systematic theology is to make rational statement of Christian belief. That belief is its raw material, and it has therefore to work with an idea of what its content is. Of course modern systematic theology (where it is found!) is often well aware of change and development in Christian belief over the centuries and of its inevitable conditioning by the cultural situations in which it is expressed. Yet the dominant pressure is bound to be towards the discerning of continuities, even towards a sort of conditioned timelessness. The datum of revelation, however defined in mode and content, is not an entity to be bypassed. As datum, it holds at arm's length historical enquiry that seeks to go beyond a certain point of usefulness. History is its servant. So, for example, it is inclined to work with 'the Trinity' as a given doctrine. This doctrine will be discerned, albeit in rudimentary form, in scripture: in the New Testament, if not in the Old. Its development will be outlined. It can be recognized as existing in different forms; it can be re-examined and re-stated in new intellectual environments. Nevertheless, it is an 'it', an identifiable and essentially single object, simply there, as it undergoes these various developments while remaining itself – a slow-change artist whose changes of outward vesture do not affect the real self inside the costumes.

Enquiry of a primary historical kind is bound to see the matter in other terms.[3] If it investigates the origins of Christian belief, it sees it in its complex – and to us alien – setting, of already existing belief and of cultural and social circumstance. In that first context of Christian faith, itself far from homogeneous, it can distinguish ways in which belief concerning God was expressed. Those ways include the person and role of Jesus, seen as representing God and speaking and acting centrally on his behalf. They also include varied and not always consistent styles of language about the Spirit – all of them, in their diversity, understandable against the background of Jewish usage, and some of them linked, in a variety of ways, to discourse about Jesus and God's work in him. It is not natural – without anachronism and without thinking of the subsequent story – to speak of these ways of expressing belief as constituting, or even necessarily entailing or adumbrating, the trinitarian doctrine. Such historical enquiry sees 'the doctrine of the Trinity' as a belief, variously conceived and expressed, which came to consciousness, first obscurely but with increasing definition, during the second century, and even then is thought of in a number of different patterns of ideas which are in some ways at variance with each other, though all are intelligible in the philosophical context of the period. There may then be the question whether its various forms (e.g. in the Cappadocian Fathers and Augustine) are really best seen as versions of the same doctrine or as distinct ways of reflecting on certain central aspects of Christian experience, which only from a distance can plausibly be seen as essentially one. 'The doctrine' is not a datum but a product, or indeed a set of associated products.

This process of enquiry has the character, already noted, of uncovering the inner mechanism of some finished product of industry which is presented for public view, or revealing the hidden devices whereby an evening of theatrical spectacle is created.[4] Such uncovering involves a loss of innocence for new initiates and they may wish to count the cost before they allow themselves to experience it. The marvel of the machine or the magic of the play will no longer be what they were. But understanding will be enhanced, even if by way of painful and unwelcome compensation.

So to see how ideas which eventually contributed to the

doctrine of the Trinity had their origin – differently shaped and motivated then – is to shed the sense of that doctrine as simply given. To know how it 'works' is to strip it of a certain kind of impressiveness and power, and inevitably to relativize what may have seemed hitherto an essentially timeless belief, even when its constituents and variations were perceived to take their place in numerous different contexts of belief. To know how it works is also to be made sceptical about the drawing of theological or devotional inferences from the doctrine which assume it as datum, as in effect (rarely, in avowal) descriptive of God's being, as somehow transcending the mechanism which makes it work, rather than as one means (that established in the patristic period where its mechanism really belonged) of giving intellectual organization to Christian experience.

Religious commitment, like systematic theology within the sphere of theological study, resists such probing behind the scenes or taking to bits of the machine, with the added motive of reverence for the sacred. It is deeply inimical to the rigorous historical objectifying which we have had in mind. The impropriety seems self-justifying and not even to require formal backing from theories of revelation. In that respect, the reaction of religious commitment is distinguishable from that of systematic theology, even though in practice it may often act to reinforce it.

Here once more there is an obstinate divergence of sensibility between devotion and study. The gap seems unbridgeable. How big a price in either religious or theological adaptability may rightly be paid for trying to bridge it? That seems to be the key question. It may be that just as the study of a play may increase and not ruin our enjoyment of a visit to the theatre, so understanding of how beliefs arose and developed, in the manner envisaged, may further religious perception. But there must be a price for genuine interaction: in both cases, the previous mode of understanding will change. In terms of the analogy, it may not be a question of either increasing or ruining enjoyment as currently understood, but rather of transforming the whole style of enjoyment, even of giving new meaning to the word as far as the enjoyer is concerned. A comparably profound movement may be desirable – and available – as theological study sets out to come into really candid relationship with religious commitment.

The kind of case we have just had before us directs attention to a fourth difference of sensibility created by modern theological study. It concerns the matter of anachronism.[5] An important aspect of modern historical awareness is a deep hostility to any hint of anachronism. Yet religious devotion employs it with ease and finds it in no way objectionable. To a large degree, devotion thrives on strong continuity with the long Christian past, and transports its products without ceremony into present settings as if they were native there. Such a sense of continuity-cum-simultaneity feeds devotion in many of its styles of expression, from psalms and hymns to systematic methods of prayer. For virtually the whole of the Christian period there was little or no awareness of the kinds of anachronism which now strike us so forcibly, making us recoil as figures of the past are credited with beliefs and attitudes quite alien to what we now know of their actual setting. The most familiar and far-reaching illustration is the readiness with which Jesus, both before and since serious historical enquiry into his life began, has been identified with such varied and often contradictory images and aspirations: Jesus both right-wing autocrat and left-wing revolutionary, protector of the rich and friend of the poor. George Tyrrell's well-known statement about the propensity of scholars to see in Jesus the reflection of their own ideals springs inevitably to mind.[6] Its truth is undeniable and the propensity seems ineradicable, even in sophisticated modern scholarship as it protests its capacity to avoid the trap.

But even if success in avoiding anachronism in certain matters is limited, sensitivity to it (especially in others!) is often acute and the need to flee from it is now amply recognized. Yet religious commitment finds anachronism so congenial that the question arises whether it can do without it. To resume the example of Jesus: if we are resolutely to exclude any understanding of him which goes beyond the context of life in first-century Galilee, how can a sense of his universality, of his transcending time and place, survive? Can we make him 'our Jesus' and can he identify with us? What can it mean to appeal to the living Jesus and invoke his support for causes far outside the ken of first-century Galileans? Conversely, if we believe in the living Jesus, are we to see him as tied for eternity to views (e.g. on divorce, poverty, or the state) which he once expressed in his earthly life so long ago? Frankly, is Jesus permitted to be relative and to change his mind? Once more, the gap seems unbridgeable between the two styles of sensibility; once more, the question must arise, whether the issue is correctly posed, or whether it might be put otherwise, in ways that give us a better chance of arriving at a whole and unfragmented mind.

These differences of sensibility between theological study and religious commitment do not necessarily amount to total incompatibilities, though certain ways of presenting them or certain aspects of them may reach that point, so that the rational person who feels their force is even driven to despair of progress. They can be seen partly and importantly as psychological contraries: as they present themselves they include strong intellectual aspects, but their effect is wider than a person's natural concern to reach a harmony of ideas and beliefs; it reaches out to his or her sense of direction, even of identity. The area of thought and experience concerned naturally brings with it this width of involvement. For particular individuals (and sometimes for whole communities), the situation may be crisis-laden.

Not all whose experience leads them to share the interests discussed in this book will recognize themselves in the depiction of all these aspects of sensibility where study and commitment to faith come into tension or conflict. It is quite possible to be aware of only some of them. Nevertheless, all belong together. This is so not just in the sense that all are interconnected and are now found in the experience of religious people who engage in theological study, but also by virtue of the fact that all may profitably be 'treated' along similar lines and in the light of certain basic considerations. It is proper to speak in terms of treatment, for there is a question of profitless and destructive pain and of the desirability of a cure in the hope of releasing new energies. There can be little doubt that the present situation is unhealthy, whether because those who experience tension find themselves settling for compromises and accommodations which they feel to be unsatisfactory or dishonest, or because the situation leads some, who are initially disposed, never to embark seriously on theological study or to engage themselves religiously, out of apprehension concerning the difficulties they see ahead.

There is one fundamental realization which may begin to open the door towards the overcoming of the difficulties which have been outlined. It concerns the degree of clarity and finality legitimately to be expected in the formation of religious and theological understanding. Pervasively and from its very roots, Christian consciousness is two-sided on this matter. There are strong impulses towards definition and assurance of certainty; other impulses (perhaps more deep than strong) towards tentativeness and provisionality. For the former side, we go back to the proclamatory element in the presentation of Jesus' mission in the Gospels: he speaks and acts with urgency and authority.[7] In the background lies the authoritative quality in the work of the classical prophets of Israel. Those beginnings were continued in beliefs concerning the apostolic mission of the church.[8] They were fortified by the emergence of creeds and the defining activities of councils and popes, which, while often limited and negative in purpose (to exclude error rather than to fix truth), nevertheless created a strong presumption in favour of belief as known, stable and unshifting. All the forces in church life concerned with matters of power and authority have always served to strengthen these impulses: non-theological in origin and nature, they push congenial theological concerns further along their established path and add to their attractiveness. Some of them have been positively irreligious, such as the crude desire to eliminate opponents, but they have still played their part, and genuinely theological or religious beliefs on this side have clothed barbarous cruelty with the sanctions of piety.

The other side finds early expression in the parabolic character of Jesus' teaching,[9] and more widely in the image-filled, non-propositional and non-philosophical nature of the biblical literature in general. Even writings like the Gospel of John, which later came to play a prominent part in propositional definition in Christian theology, do not warrant and cannot bear that evaluation of their original intention and mentality.[10] Here, whether implicity or explicitly, it is a matter of imagery, styles of perception and religious awareness, offered for sharing and appropriation. It is of their very nature that such presentations of belief will be taken up in different ways according to the capacity and outlook of those who receive them. They invite constant development along fresh lines. The New Testament itself shows how quickly they received it.[11]

Just as the proclamatory tendency was strengthened and at the same time given new shape in the process of the fixed formulation and the definition of theological ideas, so the tentative and open tendency was presented anew in the patristic period, in a philosophically rooted form, in the negative theology characteristic of much Eastern Christian thought: God is beyond human comprehension and thought of in terms of negative rather than positive attributes.[12] The doctrine of the incarnation served to resolve some of the tension between this impulse and its competitor: the transcendent God who is beyond human power to describe had, in Christ, become open to human encounter and human grasp, and indeed by his redemptive act man himself had been raised to the level of heaven – human nature itself had been divinized.[13] Nevertheless, however dramatic and lofty the concept of Christ's saving work, there always remained the inaccessibility and 'otherness' of God in himself, the space, at least potentially, for provisionality in human attempts to speak of God and certainly for growth in human knowledge of God and closeness to him. It is necessary to repeat that this impulse, more deep than strong, has always come second in public esteem in Christian life viewed as a whole. It has been stronger in monasteries than in synods, among obscure and weak Christians than among prominent and powerful Christians. It has been a major and fertile inspiration, but proved hard to use in many areas of practice. Often, it has virtually faded from sight.[14]

Both these impulses, so contrary yet so long present together in Christianity, have their modern forms of expression. The former is not essentially different in its manifestations from what is has traditionally been. It is after all so bound up with verbally static authorities and with deliberate dependence on the past that only small (and usually unacknowledged) movement is likely. There is inevitably adaptation to changed settings, but this is, in matters deemed significant, unconscious or unwanted. It is, for example, commoner for those attached to catholic Christianity to bring out the solidarity of succession in the episcopate and its doctrinal importance than to note the vast differences between holders of the episcopal office from one time and place to another. Sometimes, however, this adaptation to new settings or climates of thought and feeling can be of great interest, as when a whole area of authoritatively backed belief slips almost unnoticed from view, or indeed into view; as in the former case with the present shift to the margins of common Christian concern of once central and anxiety-ridden subjects related to the Last Things (especially the most unpleasant ones, judgment, purgatory and hell, but even heaven and life after death itself), and in the latter case with the firmer prominence given to Marian dogmas in the century from the 1850s and the recent papal espousal of universal human rights, a concept which was far from winning the support of earlier popes. Nevertheless, where the authoritative impulse is felt, a high degree of official unchangingness is to be expected.

The second impulse, that towards tentativeness in definition and provisionality in expressing awareness of God who is essentially unknowable, is at a disadvantage in a secularized environment, and the objectifying tendencies of theological study only increase its disability further. In such an environment, where religious commitment feels under pressure, the assertive, proclamatory impulse comes to the fore. There seems to be no place for what appears to be the luxury of hesitation or rumination in coming to the statement of belief – even when religious motives are involved. To admit dissatisfaction with or limitations in the value of tried, traditional modes of belief is to invite the charge of weakness or even treason to the cause. All too easily, this impulse loses its religiousness and slides, discouraged, into unbelief. It is not too much to say that, in a secularized setting, forces that might once have made for contemplative, unstrident faith tend instead towards the rejection of formal religious belief. In some cases, even in the midst of avowed atheism, the contemplative religious spirit remains and finds new ways of flourishing.[15] These cases are at present rare, and whether they represent a marginal, maverick strain in Christian forms of life, a position which has little chance of achieving stability, or foreshadow a slimmed-down style of Christianity which will become widespread in the Western world, only time will tell. For the moment, we may see them as representing a one-sided way of bringing the two impulses into a kind of harmony. In that sense, the contemplative spirit shares the concerns expressed in this book.

Is there, however, a way of giving expression to the provisionalizing impulse which offers more hope of meeting the needs of those who feel a disjunction of sensibility between theological study and religious commitment? We have seen that modern theological study inevitably works with a sense of the limitedness of particular historical situations and the beliefs and ideas to be found within them. It gives weight to the distinctive and the local, even at the expense of the shared and the universal. It brings out discontinuities and is acutely sensitive to anachronism. It is sceptical about claims to represent unchanging tradition and timeless faith. Given a certain spiritual courage, there is not a very great distance between this cluster of theological attitudes and a religious recognition of God's otherness and essential unknowability and of the necessary tentativeness of human speech about him. This is not by any means an acknowledgment of the futility or falsity of human speech about God or an admission that all our beliefs are equally useless as pointers to him, with one idea being as good or bad as any other; it is not even a denial of the revelatory principle that, by this agency or that, God makes himself known to man. It is simply a recognition of the culturally conditioned nature of all our beliefs and so of the limitedness of our speech about God. It puts brakes on the confidence with which we make religious claims, creates a mood of suggestion rather than assertion, of willingness to learn from others rather than determination only to teach; and it moves the emphasis off theological statement as the most solid and prestigious (at least among the theologically educated) form of religious utterance and opens the way to seeing other kinds of Christian expression (e.g. the generous acceptance and undemanding love to be found in some Christian groups) as closer to the heart of the matter.

In such a spirit, there is room to recognize not only that the styles of sensibility engendered by modern theological study are not hostile to religious commitment but that they are positively amenable to it, once the truth and value in the provisionalizing impulse are appreciated. There must, however, be the courage to which I referred. It will not do to move towards openness to this impulse and then to retreat when sensitive points of belief (different for different individuals and groups) are reached. The principle has to be accepted and acted upon consistently, if it is to help us to achieve the purpose of reaching a unified Christian mind. Integration is jeopardized when the quest for it is hesitant and limited. So it is inadmissible to have sticking-points – beliefs which are regarded as immune from the conditions of historical existence (i.e. development, changes of inner shape as well as outward expression, and being enmeshed with the various cultural settings in which they are held) or as articles by which the faith stands or falls.

For some, the resurrection of Jesus has this status: where this is not believed, there Christian faith is not held. Yet theological study yields no agreement which can overcome the historical obscurity and the variety of doctrinal understanding which surround it. Of course firm convictions are held about one or another historical or doctrinal view: but the agenda is open, and reasonable people contribute to a scene where uncertainty is simply 'there' and where diversity of understanding cannot be wished away, however loudly any particular opinion may assert itself. Where evidence is open to scrutiny and there are criteria for the weighing of evidence, mere assertion and testimony do not suffice.[16]

But supposing it to be recognized that this is the state of affairs with which faith must now reckon, then the realization may come that a religion which depended absolutely upon any such uncertain tenet concerning God and his expression of himself towards us would have both lost the possibility of assured truth espoused by some and abandoned the sense of God as knowable only in part and by limited human means espoused by others. It would have fallen foul of both the contrary impulses which we have discussed.

The same status may be occupied by the doctrine of the Trinity, or by a version of the classical pattern of christology, or else by the infallibility of scripture or of the papal office, or by the necessity of the historic episcopate in the church's structure. But in all cases, theological study yields the same cautions: these beliefs are not unchanging, stable rocks in a sea of shifting and developing human beliefs and notions. They are themselves, despite the continuing names by which they are identified, within the swirling waters, and the names are to a large degree convenient labels whereby a body of related but distinct ideas and institutions may be recognized. The Platonizing instinct which leads people to speak of '*the* doctrine of the Trinity', or '*the* apostolic succession', as if laid up in heaven, is bound to give way in the face of historical awareness. It is my present contention that religious commitment need show no fear in accepting the change.

– 4 –

Putting Things Together

Dissatisfaction with many of the developments described in the last two chapters is not often brought to the surface, and attempts to overcome their disquieting effects are far too rare. They receive nothing like the theological attention given to the related but more limited subjects of the interpretation of the Bible and, especially in Catholic theology, to the interpretation of other doctrinal authorities; yet they are of the utmost importance to the broad hermeneutical task.

In fact, some traditional aspects of the two interpretative operations to which I have just referred fall away in the face of them, as in the following example. It is now not uncommon to find studies of aspects of Christian understanding in matters of doctrine or ethics which set out to combine the use of historical criticism in handling the Bible with an assumption of the authority of the Bible as a doctrinal datum, upon which Christian commitment depends.[1] In such cases, the hermeneutical problem resolves itself into the question: how may that authority (taken as normative) be understood, given a historical understanding of the text and an awareness of modern thought and circumstances? Or: by what means may the Bible's normative quality find expression? But, supposing the normative role of the Bible is itself seen as a product of certain identifiable situations and processes in Christian experience – not as a fixed star in the Christian firmament, but subject to a scrutiny which reveals the pressures under which it

38

arose and the variety of forms it has taken – how then are we to
regard studies in doctrine or ethics of the kind described? The
effect of such moves is to push behind the Bible and the idea of
its authority to a realization of the deeper and more comprehensive issues which have come before us in this book.

Similarly, doctrinal authorities exist, in the conditions of
modern enquiry, not only to be interpreted but to be interrogated. Their credentials are subject to historical questioning
and evaluation. We simply know (or know that it is possible to
know) the mixed and complex pedigree of the ideas which
contributed to the christological formulations of the church's
early centuries. The central christological issue as traditionally
stated (how Jesus can be understood as both human and
divine) is not a timeless presence in Christianity, simply
provided from outside: its origins and background are known,
other and earlier ways of reacting to Jesus are known; as are the
reasons why an issue arose in the stated form and why it
became central. So it can no longer be seen as fundamental, as
bedrock, so far as Christian thought is concerned. There is that
which lies deeper, and it is itself a development, one reaction
among others to a number of describable forces; one way,
determined by circumstances, of expressing Christian experience.[2] So it is with all authoritative doctrinal formulations,
including those of more recent times, where the ecclesiastical
and cultural influences on their formation are more accessible
and perhaps more readily recognized.

In none of these cases is it a matter of saying that the loss of
innocence undeniably brought by historical enquiry leads to
the rejection of beliefs previously held. There is no necessary
link between the explanation of a historical process and a
judgment about truth. To come to understand the process
whereby classical christological doctrine, or the doctrine of
Mary's assumption, arose is not of itself to give up adherence to
them. It is, however, a matter of finding one's way of adhering
to them transformed, even of coming to a new understanding of
what adherence means. It is to be aware of their place in a wider

context of belief and to see through the particular conceptual pattern, dependent on a specific conceptual context, to the underlying religious awareness which it represents. It may, of course, (the risk is inevitable) lead to the realization that the pedigree of a particular belief is such that disbelief rightly ensues, for it turns out to rest upon little more than historical invention or transient and unsatisfactory patterns of thought, so that it cannot in any form properly be part of a Christian outlook but was always an aberration.[3] That canons of truth, themselves subject to scrutiny, are here overruling tradition and ecclesiastical authority is something that is inescapable. It is a condition from which theology can claim no immunity at all, and from which genuine Christian devotion to the God of truth should seek no such immunity: as if piety conferred exemptions or religion had access to absolute ways of statement and even to factual information not available to the world at large.

It is not, perhaps, surprising that attempts to promote the kind of integration demanded by the tensions and fragmentation we experience have come chiefly from those interested in the training of the clergy, though even in these circles, where the need might be thought to cry aloud, they are less common than might be expected. Both the interest and the lack of interest are understandable.

Clergy who dare to be aware of the theological and religious setting in which they work are more exposed to the present difficulties than almost anyone: it is an aspect of their professional distress in the circumstances of today. In their need to teach Christian faith to people of all kinds of education and intelligence and to give Christian witness for all kinds of situations, they have the constant task of deploying the rich but multifarious and unwieldy theological resources at their disposal. Unlike teachers, who may feel many of the same strains, they cannot retreat into the haven of objectification, simply presenting information and dropping the implications of religious commitment.

Yet, leaving out of account the incidence of obscurantism and complacency, there is another conception of the clerical position, which is full of seriousness and dignity but avoids the urgent anxiety to which the attempt to live with both theological awareness and religious commitment may give rise. If the clergy are regarded as the repositories of the tradition of theological learning, its tenants and trustees for their generation, and if their teaching role is seen as enriching the minds of others according to their capacity with this same learning, then the difficulties need not arise in anything like such an acute form. On this view, religious expression, the life of piety, is one thing; theological learning, a body of communicable information, is another. This learning is the material of the transmissible Christian culture, upon whose handing on from one generation to the next the effective survival of Christianity depends. Both the religious and the theological material are felt as 'given'. Each plays its own part, the two need not collide, and indeed a life nourished by both is rich in Christian content.

There is undoubtedly wide support for such a conception. It has the nobility and stability that come from long presence in the clerical ideal. It is often associated with a general conservatism, a stress on tradition and an optimistic perception of theological and religious continuities. Most notably, it works with an idea of theology as a body of learning and of theological formation as achieved by the acquiring of such learning. Certainly, it fails to absorb many aspects of awareness which are only too plain to those addressed in this book. It cultivates its garden, perhaps beautifully, but within walls over which it feels no call to look.

In the interests of those for whom the problematic nature of the present situation is inescapable, a certain number of proposals looking towards greater integration have been made in recent years, and I have noted that they tend to arise out of concern with the training of the clergy. It is worth making clear now that this is not the exclusive concern of this book. The challenges which the clergy face are met in other, equally disturbing, forms by others who try to combine religious commitment with open theological study. Both the difficulties and the means to their alleviation affect people in a wide range of circumstances. Indeed, one of the less helpful aspects of the situation is the way in which, until recently, theological study has been in practice too closely confined to the clergy and those training for ordination, so that the idea of it as tied to the mystery of their craft arose all too naturally – and often the concomitant idea of theology for the laity as crumbs of learning from the rich priest's table. The circumstances in view in this book are resticted to no guild. They are an element in the cultural air available to anyone to breathe – and liable to spread uninvited over lovingly constructed garden walls.

A notable proposal is to be found in the work of Edward Farley.[4] His analysis of the history and present predicament of theology is primarily concerned with clergy training, if only because the history of theological study is bound to be narrated in terms of its primary institutional purpose: but his recommendations include its release from this professional limitation. This theoretical move has been anticipated by events: in the United Kingdom at least, a great deal of formal theological study in higher education is now experienced by people whose motives and hopes are not connected with ordination or other forms of church leadership. In many cases, it is not explicitly related to life in a church setting at all, but is to be accounted for by individual rather than institutional factors.

For Farley, the widening which he advocates is still chiefly perceived in ecclesiastical terms: the extension is from leaders to led, clergy to laity, so that theological awareness is part of the common enterprise of Christian life. For theological study to serve this end, Farley sees clearly that it must overcome the fragmentation which academic developments over the past two centuries have brought about. There must be a recovery of 'theologia' as an integrated pursuit, directed towards the apprehension of the divine and the interpretation of experience in the light of God. He sees the necessity for greater variety in the way this is achieved, according to the role in life of individuals and groups, but in all cases it is empowered by 'faith', which acts as the force driving theological understanding towards integration in the outlook of those who experience it. With these intentions and hopes, the over-separate subjects, which co-exist in theological study as currently organized, can be impelled to contribute towards a single illuminative enterprise; and their overly theoretical tendency can be counteracted, in that practical Christian life is in view throughout.

It is pardonable (in that he is so much a lone voice) that Farley's analysis of the predicament of theological study, especially when viewed with the needs of those training for church leadership (widely interpreted) in mind, is more compelling than his remedies. His general proposals are unexceptionable, but their level of generality is high, and more work is needed to translate them into practical steps intellectually and educationally. There is too a neglect of those factors, deep in the disturbed consciousness of many, which we have identified under the heading of the alienation of theology from religion. In that way, Farley is too sanguine. Somehow or other, ways need to be found of doing adequate justice to the twin concerns of those who feel devoted to the claims of both modern theological study, as part of available truth, and religious commitment, as that which gives basic meaning to existence in a way that nothing else can.

Not dissimilar ideas have recently come to the fore among some of those more directly responsible for the training of the clergy.[5] Again we observe that this limitation of interest is both natural and unfortunate. Natural, for it is here that the shoe pinches, especially for church authorities faced with complaints about the lack of effectiveness and the relevance to practical ministry of current programmes of theological study; unfortunate in that the continuing concentration on this group of students and, whatever their special needs, their isolation from others engaged in theological study is increasingly artificial and makes for distortion and impoverishment. Theology is no longer usefully seen as chiefly the technical equipment of the clerical profession.

From this source, the plea is once more for some means whereby the discrete disciplines of theological study can be made to interact and contribute to the formation of an integrated theological outlook. There is a growing sense of division between theology as taught in secular institutions of higher education and the needs of those engaged in theological study with church leadership and practical ministry in view. Is it possible to develop new ways of study which can maintain academic integrity yet avoid capitulating to ideology or the cult of edifying generalities, and arrive at honest and usable theological understanding? In other words, can the present monopoly of the traditional and yet problem-ridden procedures of theological study be broken, especially when those who alone might be able to break it, and are likely to be aware of its weaknesses, have been trained to work only in accordance with them and to value their manifest achievements?

In a few quarters involved in this sector of theological study, there is discernible a movement towards seeing that study along quite other than traditional lines of organization. It is a matter of calling upon areas of human experience (e.g. work, family, political loyalty, death) to provide the agenda, while the traditional disciplines provide some of the tools. At present, it might be said, the disciplines provide the agenda, while human experience provides some of the material which they use. In the new arrangement, the agenda is closer to the ways in which theological questions arise in life, and it is easier to see how concerns conventionally hived off into 'doctrine' or 'ethics' or 'spirituality' actually form wholes as they enter into a person's experience. In this context, the church leader is regarded not simply as a custodian and repository of Christian culture but as one who can be called upon to interpret and illuminate life in the light of Christian understanding.

If that role is to be played on the basis of more than well-intentioned hunches, then intellectual attention needs to be given formally to this new-style agenda for theological study. At present, the pastor who wishes to 'interpret and illuminate life' and is dissatisfied with learned recourse to Bible and tradition as giving him sufficient resources has little practical alternative but to resort to a combination of secular analysis and theological commonplaces. There is little experience of problem-centred theological enquiry compared with the vast array of work devoted to the traditional disciplines. Yet, in life, theological problems do not present themselves in terms of those disciplines, but by way of situations which demand theological interpretation. The starting-point is in experience. The deliverances of the traditional disciplines provide the raw material for such interpretation, but they are not in themselves equipped to carry investigation further. Thus, what is still far from clear when this approach to theological study is adopted is how the raw material can be processed in order to arrive at judgments which do justice to the situation or area in question, to religious commitment and to significant theological understanding.

The standard report of church working-parties on social or moral issues illustrates the difficulty. Works in this genre often begin with an outline of such Old Testament and New Testament evidence and then material from Christian history as may be thought relevant to the matter in hand. Usually, the material is treated historically according to critical principles. The outline draws upon the conventional disciplines of study, though it often presents its material in theological guise as 'the witness of the tradition'. There follows an account of the present predicament which has prompted the setting-up of the working-party, and finally a reasoned and enlightened judgment which accords with the views of most of those in the population who are *bien pensant*. What is not always apparent is the reasoning whereby movement has taken place from the material drawn from the academic disciplines (itself usually

45

full of variety and contradiction) to the ultimate recommendations concerning the present state of affairs. It may be that certain major thrusts can be identified running through all the evidence produced: even so, is that homogeneity to be seen as determinative for present judgment and by what criteria may there still be work to do in the light of new circumstances? At this point the situation is deeply uncertain. The more realistically the biblical and historical material is viewed in context, the less prescriptive and even illuminating it can be. The account of the present state of affairs, intelligently analysed in terms of the relevant tools of study, then comes to be given in largely secular terms, and it is hard to see how a significantly theological judgment can take place. Hence there is nothing surprising about the tendency for such enquiries, starting from an area of human experience, whether conducted by churches or by students, to end up in a pale theological colouring of enlightened opinion. The foregoing description contains an element of caricature. It casts no slur on the high quality of work found in the several parts of such documents. Its complaint is about the procedure as a whole. For that to be satisfactorily carried out we are short of skill.

In basic principle, then, the enterprise represented by this procedure is admirable and it is the execution which lacks sophistication. There would be benefit if more formal academic work could be developed, in order to make the wheels of interaction between diverse areas of enquiry and perception run more smoothly. Initially, it would be a matter of cooperative, inter-disciplinary work; but it might lead to a rearrangement of the traditional way of dividing up the territory of theological work, with new titles for professorships and new approaches to the content of examinations. The advantage in view here is chiefly for those keen to bring theological study and religious commitment into genuine relationship. But the obstacles are formidable: in the experiential areas to which such a method is most likely to be applied, it is hard to see signs of genuinely theological movement from a set of interesting contributions from the traditional disciplines, all of which speak with such distinct and uncollaborative voices.

None of the approaches so far considered, at least as conducted at present, gets close enough to the interaction which is required. The relation between religious commitment and theological study which they encourage is valuable as far as it goes, but thorough interaction is hardly the right way to describe it. Even when the will is present, as for example in a close-knit specialist working-party or a friendly university department, the mind or heart falters. The conflicts of sensibility described in the last chapter are scarcely affected even if something is done to unify the theological disciplines. It is possible that the proposals I have mentioned are all too ambitious and too monolithic. Our ills may be too complex and too diversely felt to admit of a single omnibus cure. Those whose studies have taken the form of a relatively superficial but balanced introduction to a range of theological subjects are well placed to know the problems, but badly placed to achieve the thorough integration of outlook and redirection of understanding which is desired. They lack experience and sureness of touch, though they will come to make their own partial and limited essays in integration as opportunity offers and life demands. Of course they must not be deterred from such movement, but there is bound to be stumbling and the taking of fruitless paths. They are not in a position, if they proceed along such a wide front, to build soundly or to lead others. On the other hand, the established expert in a particular field is often unbalanced by reason of his very expertness. Through concentration on one area, his knowledge and judgment in others have become outdated and unreliable, and, as we have seen, his capacity for intelligibility or cogency in relation to colleagues in other subjects is often limited. Nevertheless, he has standing and confidence. His assurance in his own field is a major asset. It can provide the basis for prudent plans aimed to further the purposes which we have in mind. It gives him a position to offer leadership to others, who see the need but are too inexperienced to act unaided.

There is much to be said for developing the task in mind along a number of different lines, each taking one of the major disciplines, viewed critically, as its starting-point. In this way, the most can be made of the strengths of present practice. The question then becomes: if we take seriously the results of study of the chosen subject, how may we move towards a formation of mind and then of life which does justice to those results and does not belie them? The strength of this approach is in the area of reducing the alienation of theology from religion. Of itself, it does not do much to reduce the fragmentation within theological studies and the sad effects of the ignoring of the fruits of work in one field by those working in another. Nevertheless, it should create a presumption that those effects are to be faced. So, taking a subject-based approach as meritorious because it is practical, we have to add the further requirement: it is a matter of not only taking the results of the study of the chosen subject seriously, but also making every effort not to ignore results in other fields, even if the skill for doing so is not readily to hand.

Thus, liturgists should aim not to use the Bible as if historical criticism had never come upon the scene; doctrinal and ethical studies need to be consistently aware that biblical scholars and historians have made accessible the context and pedigree of doctrinal and ethical ideas; church historians need to keep in their sights the hermeneutical implications of the story they disclose; and biblical scholars should be alive to the possibilities for doctrinal thinking that are implicit in their work.[6] In nearly every case, it is, in one way or another, a matter of asking for the mutual awareness of two kinds of theological endeavour: the abstract and the historical, each prone to underplay the importance of the other; the one inclined (while denying it) to work with a sense of the timelessness of ideas, the other inclined (while denying it) to see historical discovery and elucidation as a self-justifying and self-sufficient activity without further implication; the one seemingly edging towards

48

religious commitment, the other seemingly moving away from it in a spirit of deliberate detachment. The phrase 'while denying it' is included as a sign of hope that the plea for mutual awareness may be accepted, despite the undoubted difficulty of acting on it – at least as a brake on some of the procedures commonly found in the traditional fields of study.

If we find sense in the proposal that it is wise to take one established discipline of theological study as the starting-point, then choice must be made. The present enquiry is then required to narrow its scope. So far it has ranged widely over the theological and religious fields, having in view its particular audience. But if progress is to be made, the range needs to be reduced, even though that means paying a price: only a proportion of those who might have shared the argument so far will want to make the same choice and so feel able to identify with what follows. The cost is offset by the fact that the discipline chosen is only a starting-point, and by the openness to other subjects which we see as obligatory, if the object in view is to be achieved. In that sense, the narrowing is only a necessary first step: one starts somewhere only because one cannot start everywhere. At the same time, the starting-point is intended, as we have seen, to determine the continuing direction. It recognizes that people's interests and activities are limited and specific, even if they are also urged to transcend their limitations in the interests of the goal that is sought.

The subject I have chosen here is the study of the New Testament. So our question now has this form: if we take modern study of the New Testament seriously, how may we look on the theological task as a whole and how are we to view our religious commitment? There are good objective reasons for making this choice and recommending it to others. The New Testament is the earliest source for Christian belief and is the deepest layer in its structure of authority. Concern with the New Testament is closely connected to all other areas of Christian theology and utterly bound up with Christian commitment. Doctrine, ethics and liturgy are distinct fields of

49

study, but as traditionally pursued they include a New Testament component. In that sense at least, the study of the New Testament has a fundamental, even normative role in theological study as a whole.

New Testament studies offer an essential inroad to central Christian questions, and in some cases the only possible inroad: Who was Jesus? What did he stand for? What is his significance, historically and in relation to God? At the same time, it is common knowledge that the fruits of the study of the New Testament offer some of the most disturbing and far-reaching challenges to traditional Christian belief. Of all areas of theological study, this is the one which arouses most anxiety from the point of view of religious commitment. It is here that 'tampering with the sacred' is most apparent. It is to be expected that taking New Testament studies as our starting-point will lead to a re-focussing of both our understanding of Christian belief and our perception of Christian commitment. It is hard to think of any other starting-point which would bring before us more starkly the issues with which this book is concerned.

We cannot reckon that the process of genuine integration of outlook will leave us unchanged, or even leave unchanged our grasp of the very nature of religious commitment. Is our adherence to God himself or to valued ways of thinking about God; to the Christian cause or to cherished expressions of Christian life? Thus, in the very act of deciding to set our chosen academic subject of New Testament studies to work in this unaccustomed way, we already begin to make it perform a salutary religious function – sniffing out areas where we are content to settle for ideas or images of God, giving up the quest for God himself. The task we are undertaking has its iconoclastic aspect as well as its constructive purposes.

There is another reason why the choice of the study of the New Testament has a peculiarly nettle-grasping character. The smallness of the quantity of the New Testament writings, together with their cruciality in Christian thought and life, means that many of the difficulties which I have brought forward arise in this area with special force. It is here that many traditional doctrines have their roots, so that the question arises: do the historical origins of Christianity warrant or sustain the beliefs which, as a matter of fact, they were taken to have generated and which have always been thought to depend upon them? It is perhaps here that the very intensity of study has brought to sharpest awareness the alienness of the earliest Christians from ourselves and the discontinuities between them and us, and indeed between them and their closer successors in the patristic period which followed them.

Our first step is to note that the realization of alienness and of discontinuities rules out certain instinctive ways of proceeding, and in particular cautions us to work obliquely. Faced with the task of using the New Testament in the business of building an integrated theological outlook and fostering Christian commitment, yet not forswearing knowledge of its historically conditioned quality, the natural impulse is to look for broad thrusts[7] of early Christian belief which are to carry weight with us, even when the details of their outlook are plainly no longer convincing or applicable. Thus, we doubt the direct utility to us of their speculations about the imminent end of the world, but we should continue to feel the authority of their ethic centred on love. The danger here is not only the almost overwhelming tendency to select as 'broad thrusts' those aspects of early Christian belief that are either congenial to us or susceptible of fairly direct application; but also a failure to see that their thought forms a seamless robe, a whole that needs in every particular to be passed through critical filters before it can be properly received in our quite different setting. Even 'love' as understood in the first century has its place in a total outlook and is conditioned by local circumstance. It has resonances different from those felt now, and the implications of a 'love-centred ethic' are not necessarily easy to discern simply on the basis of a direct adoption of what looks like a plain imperative from the beginning of Christianity.[8]

The awareness of the New Testament 'in itself', which is perhaps the prime result of historical criticism,[9] impels us to proceed indirectly. It is a matter of following a number of lines of reflection, which share the characteristic of opening us towards wider theological implications and towards honest conditions for religious commitment; but always with an engagement to hear the New Testament speak in its own voices and not to impose upon those early writers our own religious or theological preferences.

It has been recognized throughout this book that there is something strongly subjective about the business of arriving at the integrated outlook to which it aspires. To many this is unacceptable.[10] It brings too much diversity and uncertainty into a matter where homogeneity has been highly prized. At this point in the discussion, and for the rest of this book, the subjectivity has to come into the open and disclose its terms. It should then be clearer how and when and with what limitations it is unavoidable in the present state of affairs, when it comes to the relations between theology and religion.

The subjectivity derives not only from the fact that, though we interact with each other, each must make his or her own links, but also from the need to choose between starting-points, which is almost forced upon us by the present situation. Furthermore, the approach adopted here will not readily yield ordered and uniform propositional belief of the traditional kind. The propositional expression of belief, for example in creeds, began either as a summary of belief, useful for purposes such as baptism where such a summary was required, or as a set of defining articles to stand by in case of challenge or uncertainty. The continued usefulness of this kind of expression of belief is now restricted to the former role. Belief has its roots elsewhere and takes other outward forms; creeds and the like are a convenient summary, no more. They are not a final court of appeal but useful pointers, in certain contexts, to that which lies deeper. Those deeper expressions of belief are more personal, more fluid, closer to experience, inevitably more subjective. There is, of course, no question of denying the existence or the value of consensus or overlap; rather of recognizing that the springs of belief are at a level which formal statements are inadequate to express.[11]

We cannot finish this consideration of the choice of starting-point without a final glance at the narrowing necessarily involved. In taking the New Testament as our beginning, we take on the balance of the New Testament's concerns and its boundaries. It does not start at the roots of religious belief or consider belief in orderly, conceptual terms, as modern study of theology requires. There are, therefore, many questions which this starting-point leads us to neglect, and interests which we are led to assume rather than to argue for from scratch: such as the centrality of God, the strength of his purpose, and the setting of it all in the light of Jesus.

In the next chapter we turn to the question: starting from the study of the New Testament and taking it seriously as part of the truth before us, in what directions are we to travel, especially with regard to Christian believing?

-5-

Starting from the New Testament

The best that individuals can offer is their own attempt at the task of integration. It will be limited by training and interests, but any more far-reaching ambition is likely to be grandiose and impractical. So the appeal will be particularly to those who have shared a person's starting-point and something like his or her own pattern of study. They will not necessarily accept this way of attempting a unified theological outlook, but at least they will be able to follow the course of the reflection and feel the force of the difficulties it seeks to meet. This attempt starts from a point familiar in one degree or another to the greater number of those who have received an education in theology, whether in university or elsewhere: that formed, at least in part, by a detailed historical study of the Bible and the New Testament in particular.

At no point in the whole range of Christian theological studies do so many different kinds of factors combine to produce difficulty and anxiety. Not only are there severe academic problems, both literary and historical, admitting few settled solutions and all the more nagging because the territory is small and inimical to generalization; but many of these problems relate, intricately but inevitably, to issues of faith and commitment. They will not stay in their academic box – the study of the New Testament in itself – but slip out constantly into territory officially annexed by other disciplines, such as 'doctrine' or 'systematic theology'.

Apart from those whose starting-point is in New Testament studies, there are other groups of theological enquirers to whom this investigation is of importance: people whose imaginative and intellectual starting-point is in other studies than the New Testament still often find themselves facing the results of New Testament studies as they build up their picture of theology as a whole. It is scarcely too much to say that, within the now immense range of Christian studies, all of them having, from a phenomenological standpoint, their right to living-space, New Testament studies cannot avoid sooner or later exercising a kind of imperialism. Highly technical though they have so largely become, they may at any moment be called upon to emerge from their own enclosure and, all unprepared, form relations with other kinds of Christian enquiry. This might, indeed, be expected to occur more often than it does.

At first sight, this is so obvious as to be hardly worth saying; but there are at least two points of view which make it necessary to bring it out explicitly. First, it is held by some that the documents of Christian origins should cease to play any other than a purely historical role in Christian theology. Christianity now should be a response to present circumstances, in line with present opportunities and constraints, not a system of belief warranted or even necessarily inspired by the faith and arrangements of those far-off days. Of course, to be recognizable as Christianity, it must include certain thrusts of belief and attitude which derive ultimately from that distant source, but, the circumstances and possibilities for belief being now so different, even these will now take a quite different form, and certain major aspects of New Testament belief (notably eschatology) will scarcely feature at all or, if they still appear, it will be in a form so radically different as to be hardly capable of being identified, at least without unconvincing ingenuity, with the remote New Testament ancestor. In traditional theological terms, this may be characterized as a radical 'Spirit' theology: its focus is clearly on 'God in the present'.

Second, many Christians, who would be far from accepting

55

such a viewpoint as the basis for a doctrinal position, go a long way towards working with it in practice. They may even be fervent in their formal allegiance to traditional doctrine, including its New Testament foundations. They may, using interpretative processes which seem to them satisfactory, actually believe that they derive their faith from the New Testament witnesses and insist on New Testament warrants for their policies. Yet it is not difficult to show how far they really are from the perspectives of the New Testament and how little their beliefs enter into the reality of those first Christian beliefs. And of course there are others who, more superficially, affirm solidarity with New Testament faith but make little serious attempt to conform to its contents or its proportions of emphasis. In practical terms, they are in a position not much different from those described in the last paragraph, who at least have the merit of being candid. In effect, their theological horizon is created by present ecclesiastical or social needs, just as those more theoretically minded are moved by present intellectual pressures and constraints.

To those who reach such a conviction on serious and deliberate grounds, it is necessary to outline with some care the position to be claimed for the New Testament at this stage in the discussion. It is certainly not that it is, with whatever interpretative subtlety, determinative for present belief: historical sensibility rules that out, as it is exercised both in the understanding of the particularities of New Testament beliefs and the life of the early churches and in the appreciation of the present context for belief. But also it is not that the New Testament is a matter of indifference for us, or simply, as a matter of mere fact, the first stage in that process of theological development which may now seem just to wend its way through time and, clean contrary to its constant claims, to sit loose to any genuine appreciation of original belief. Rather, it is a question of perceiving the nature of the nexus between the fount of Christian belief in the earliest period and the subsequent developments. It simply is the case that, with what now seems a large degree of anachronistic failure to see the New Testament writers' beliefs in their terms[1], their successors based themselves on these New Testament writers – not as mere predecessors but as authorities, as 'scripture'. More, the nexus between the New Testament and what followed presents us with a kind of pure specimen for examining the question of Christian development. Here the process may be examined, contemplated and considered, for both its nature and its content, in a pristine form, and conclusions concerning method and procedure arrived at.

But further, the continual recurrence to this earliest period by all subsequent Christian theologies, even though usually in ways that now seem inadequate or even bizarre, renders it impossible to do other than accept the need to face it 'in itself' in the process of arriving at a unified theological picture. And there is no reason to suppose that Christians can ever seriously hold on to a worthwhile religious identity without constant return to the historical figure of Jesus. Accessible only indirectly and imperfectly though he may be through the Gospel witnesses, nevertheless he must be central for realistic Christian identity, if only as enigmatic model and as critic of those Christian policies and beliefs, formed by present needs, which so easily hold the centre of the stage.

These are all more or less pragmatic reasons for the inescapability of the New Testament as a central factor in the formation of any Christian unified theological outlook. It may seem absurd that the point, put thus baldly, is one that needs to be argued for at all. What kind of Christian theology could it be that omitted or underplayed the New Testament? Yet even in theology there is such a thing as lip-service, there is formal deference to the importance of the New Testament combined with a virtual absence of any live attention to its contents and implications or will to 'listen to' it as it is now possible to listen to it. In former days, the book of the Gospels was a liturgical object, revered as such and read maybe in an alien tongue and in a chant which effectively prevented the lively appreciation of the words: it functioned more as a kind of icon, an object evoking veneration and transmitting the numinous, than as a book containing words. So, with adjustments, it may still function in the minds and habits of many who live nevertheless in a world and a church where the lively understanding of the words is 'on the agenda', available, and provided as a vital ingredient in an education in Christian theology. In many such cases, it is not that the New Testament has not been studied; it is that no way has been found – or admitted – whereby that study could affect the total theological or religious outlook. The seeming inability of many to absorb acknowledged truth about the New Testament and Christian origins into their total outlook has surely contributed substantially to the common readiness to fall back on packages of theological nostrums as a substitute for more thoughtful and defensible patterns of belief and understanding.

The study of the New Testament contributes to the building up of a total theological outlook in both approach and content. The most fundamental contribution is to induce a sense of the acceptability of diversity in Christian belief and statement. One of the clearest results of New Testament study is to force a realization of the width of Christian understanding to be found in the early church. Not, of course, that this width was a matter of policy or collusion. If anything, where it was perceived, it was strenuously fought. But looking back, we can view the diverse theologies of the first decades of Christianity in a calmer perspective. Leaving aside the acrimony which no doubt existed, we can see simply the fact of diversity and recognize a kind of historical legitimacy for all parties. It is not for us to take sides between Paul and the Letter of James, or to judge Mark in relation to Matthew's or Luke's adaptation of his work. In other words, as students of the New Testament, we feel impelled simply to let those earliest Christian thinkers 'be'; out of both scholarly detachment and a proper humility and charity towards Christian people of other circumstances than our own, facing problems which are not ours.

So this acceptance of diversity is tied to a sense of the inescapable bond between those thinkers and their times. That is where they belonged and, primarily, still belong. That is the setting in which they can be understood and weighed – if they are not to be made, in one way or another, to dance to some tune of our composing.[2] There is something unfitting when modern Christians express serious preference for Paul or John over, let us say, Matthew or the writer of the Pastoral Epistles. Of course we may feel an attraction for a particular writer, an affinity of spirit or a special admiration; but this should not weaken our ability to adopt a certain austerity towards him – to see him as belonging to his times, as one voice among the precious few whose words survive and whom we can still attempt to hear. In other words, the affinity we feel for (let us say) the teaching of Paul should not delude us into seeing him as 'really just like us', but should always be linked to a sense of his distance and difference from us and of his historical role within earliest Christianity.

This is not, as we have already seen, to adopt a thorough-going relativism. Clearly, such relativism, viewed theoretically, both cripples and negates the modern observer as he makes his judgments, and renders the one observed wholly opaque. Paul is not so completely or exclusively a man of his time that we cannot usefully enter into the business of understanding him, even though we know that our standpoint conditions the mode and content of that understanding. He is accessible, and he may or may not be found congenial; yet we owe him his distinctiveness and his place within the Christianity and the society of his day. We, who intrude into the picture we see in the very act of forming it, do much less violence and are much less likely to deceive ourselves and others if we are aware of ourselves as intruders.

The recognition of these conditions in viewing the first Christian theologies, as represented in the New Testament, forms a certain mood as we approach other, later aspects of the Christian phenomenon. What are the ingredients in that mood? It is made up of reflections such as these. Early Christianity was able to express itself in a wide variety of forms, differing to the point of contradiction, even on important issues. This diversity may not have been acceptable at the time, and certain elements within it were the subject of contention, but in retrospect it forms a total picture and each part has its own validity. Diversity seems, then, not to be of itself regrettable.[3] Christianity is a phenomenon which can bear it and thrive on it. It is, of course, another matter to deal with diversity in quite other times – when, for example, it is open to the observation of all (as, for lack of a common structure, it was not fully in New Testament times), and when there are mechanisms for exercising authority or seeking consensus; still, the diversity of the early days can induce an attitude to these later conditions which is other than that brought about by immersion in the later conditions themselves.

At this point, what was a matter of approach gives way to content. For in the light of that early diversity, certain modern pressures in doctrinal or ecclesiastical endeavour may cease to be felt so keenly – not out of indifference but out of the realization that Christianity can do very well in modes other than those of high-level agreement on formulas or explicit doctrinal statements; that Christianity is a phenomenon which need not fear seeming imprecision of statement about its beliefs but is capable of finding many different levels. In other words, certain kinds of anxiety are dispelled, and certain issues lose their cruciality. The proportions of things simply change.

It is hard, for example, given the perspective I have just described, to view the preoccupations which have chiefly dominated (and bedevilled) much ecumenical debate as worth the attention they have received. Whole 'blocks' of argument come to seem contrived – elaborate, but in the end insubstantial. Thus, the view of Christian belief which sees matters of minsterial order as 'hard' doctrine simply dissolves. It is generally rooted in a perception of New Testament times and the immediately subsequent period as having authoritative force as the fount of tradition. This involves a process of abstraction and anachronism which the whole tenor of modern New Testament study renders obsolete and unthinkable. Abstraction, in that certain limited aspects of early Christian organizational arrangements are isolated – both within the total social context and within the setting of the church itself – and given normative significance. Anachronism, in that those aspects are viewed, not in the light of their original settings but in the light of later developments; they are seen not for what they *were*, but for what, with selective and specialized hind-sight, they *led to*. It is parallel to, for example, the Shakespear-ean view of English mediaeval history, where this is viewed in the light of the eventual Tudor triumph and the Elizabethan polity.

Or if the view of matters like ministerial order as 'hard' doctrine does not depend on such an approach to tradition, then it derives from an ecclesiology which is, again, to be found in the earliest days as just one strand among several and as a response to circumstances of that time and not necessarily straightforwardly applicable to later situations. Once more, the effect is to relieve the pressure of dogmatism on the question and to shift the proportion of attention among modern Christians. Quite other matters may then appear to be now more worthy recipients of Christian energies, both intellectual and practical: matters concerned with both the conditions of man's relationship to God and its working out in the intractable social circumstances of our day. Details (as they would then be) such as how hierarchies might be united or whether women might be ordained, could then be settled by way of administra-tive tidying up! In the matter of ecumenism, high-level negotiation between churches, with their verbal agreements so barren of effect, might yield in order of evaluation to local and informal initiatives, whereby Christians, acting diversely with-out anxiety or regret, do what Christian life appears to demand of them in their situations. In large and increasing measure, this would be to recognize what is happening and to remove from it the stigma of theological 'looseness' and unease at being 'unofficial'. It would accord it a new kind of validity and dignity which might of itself promote theological seriousness.

If a capacity to grasp the place of diversity of Christian witness and thought is perhaps the most fundamental contribution which New Testament studies have to make to the formation of a total theological outlook, a second and allied contribution is a recognition of the process whereby Christian theology is brought into being and conveyed. We have already seen some of the flaws in traditional ways of understanding that process. Those ways have, with modifications and variations, concentrated on an idea of tradition[4] – of handing on a body of belief, as from teacher to pupil in an old-fashioned educational system. There may or may not be a sense of development as occurring in the process, but in either case the idea of steady transmission is central. It is, in other words, an educational model of religious communication, with a strongly didactic or instructional view of education at the heart of it. It places, implicitly, high value on safeguarding the integrity of what is believed and taught, on assurance of authority in those who teach or 'hand on', and on a willingness in those who learn simply to receive what is given.

An analysis of the origins of Christian understanding as witnessed in the New Testament points to a different way of looking at the matter, and it has repercussions for our picture of Christian understanding in any period. Moreover, it will be found to corroborate our earlier findings. This approach goes behind what New Testament writers themselves sometimes say about the process involved in tradition to the actualities.

If we consider how Christian belief, in its diversity, arose, we can postulate four key stages, each with its own distinct features. The first was the *impact* of Jesus himself. Before we even attempt to describe that impact, it is necessary to justify the use of the term. There has long been a conflict between two contrary tendencies in New Testament studies: between those whose effect is to assimilate Jesus to his Jewish environment and so to minimize his distinctiveness, and those who isolate him, even in some cases to such a degree that he seems 'a bolt from the blue' – all too ready for that docetic role in doctrine which many soon ascribed to him. Those in the former camp have the attraction of common sense and of being in some ways doctrinally fashionable: of course Jesus was a man of his time; of course he taught in terms which were intelligible to those around him, in the context of at least some aspects of first-century Judaism; of course, in order to gain any following at all, he was not outlandish but comprehensible; of course he was no divine figure *ab extra*, but a Jew whose thought-forms were bounded by the possibilities of his setting. A prominent (and unconvincing) version of this assessment points to Jesus' immersion in or reaction to the political movements of his time – how can he have been indifferent to them? – but there are many others.[5]

Those in the latter camp have the virtue of being able to account for the fact that the movement associated with Jesus survived and speedily became a significant and distinctive faith, whereas other figures in first-century Judaism, on the face of it comparable with him, left little trace. It is possible to account for this outcome unhistorically as the result of divine providence or to explain it as the effect of historical accident; but a sober historical assessment is likely to hold that there must have been that about Jesus which was distinctive and wholly memorable.[6] Those holding such a view are likely to find it insufficient, for example, to see the conviction of Jesus' distinctiveness as deriving exclusively from the resurrection or to lay the responsibility for creating real religious belief in Jesus at the feet of Paul. No, to account best for what is observable to us, the powerful distinctiveness of Jesus in the teaching and activity of his lifetime is by far the best line of explanation. So the use of the word 'impact' is legitimate. Of course he was a Jew of his time and was no culture-free divinity (if such be now imaginable), but he was nevertheless one who stood out in his teaching and in his person. To assert this we need not be sure which aspects of Jesus were distinctive: the fact of distinctiveness is enough to justify the use of the word 'impact' and to speak of that impact as the beginning of Christianity.

In no way denying the significance of the information arrayed by those who describe the background to the career of Jesus, we have seen no reason to deny either his distinctiveness. He springs indeed from an identifiable setting, but it is not unfair to see in him a new beginning, the start of a process, and this not simply with the kind of hindsight I have seen fit to deplore, but in himself, from the standpoint of his own time and place. In the career of Jesus, viewed in itself, there was enough that was new to cause a stir and to make the stir intelligible, even though there is room for disagreement where exactly the novelty lay and how great was its extent.

Indeed, the nature of that impact is strictly inaccessible to us; we cannot now know it directly or feel it for ourselves. We can only know of the fact of it – and then try to characterize the experience of which it was the cause. *Experience* is the second stage in the process whereby Christian understanding came into existence. At this stage diversity began. There was also unity – in the fact of its being the experience of Jesus' impact and of its being decisive for those who knew it. It is indeed almost tautologous to say that for all those who reacted positively to the impact of Jesus, he made 'all the difference'.[7] More dramatically, we may say that their 'world' was transformed; more technically and conventionally, that they received 'salvation'. For the renewal they experienced concerned their understanding of and relationship with God, and so also their relationship with all else in their consciousness that bore upon their dealings with him.

But here the unity ends; for salvation, or well-being in relation to God and all that relates to him, is richly diverse in its character. It is not likely to be true that what one man takes as salvation may easily be damnation to another, especially within the context of a single (though varied) culture such as first-century Judaism. Nevertheless, there can be surprising contrasts and even contradictions. Salvation relates to need, and to existing disposition and mental horizon. Capacity to experience the impact of a saviour depends upon that need and that horizon. It is *my* world and not another's which will be transformed for *me*.

Now it is clear that the impact of Jesus was experienced as bringing such salvation in certain broadly definable ways: thus, it was certainly felt and known as a liberation and as bringing reconciliation.[8] Yet each of these two major types of experience had many aspects. For some, the new sense of freedom was chiefly related to deliverance from the personal diabolical powers then widely regarded as active for ill in the world's affairs; for others, from the primacy of the law of Judaism, seen as the given means of relating to God and the chief expression of God's beneficence hitherto; for yet others, from sin or death or spiritual ignorance viewed as forces which beset man's path and ruined his happiness. And reconciliation might be the overcoming of estrangement from God or from mankind in general or within the community of fellow-believers. In some cases, we may relate the benefit to preceding lack, a need available to be met, and differing from person to person and group to group; but in others, it was only the new-found salvation which showed up the inadequacy of what preceded it. Examples of all the types just mentioned are to be found in early Christianity, sometimes in isolation, elsewhere in combination. Paul, for example, is aware of many of them, and this fact accounts substantially for the richness of his thought.[9] But the general point holds, that in the moment of receiving the impact of Jesus, people experienced him as they could and as they needed to; it was a moment wherein he and they combined – neither had a monopoly in giving content to it, neither was a mere cypher. So it is not possible to point to a particular feature and say, 'There plain and neat is the product of Jesus' hand'; or, 'There is a piece of human need which fathered its gratification on the figure of Jesus.' Each side was crucial, and each was restricted in its capacity to accomplish transformation.

I have said that the awakening of an awareness of need may follow the satisfying of it. For example, there is good reason to believe that Paul's dissatisfactions with the Jewish Law post-dated his conviction that Christ had in various crucial ways superseded it.[10] Even so, it was a matter of long-felt purposes, supremely the fulfilling of God's covenant-relationship with his people, being seen as now achieved decisively and as never before. Those purposes were part of Paul's setting and in no way outlandish.

To put it another way, certain kinds of salvation (that is, experience of well-being in relation to God) were ruled out in the time of Jesus and as possible results of his impact. Thus, no one in first-century Palestine was likely to experience him as the bringer of a Buddhist-style enlightenment or of a hope of reincarnation in some more advantageous form of life; and this not only because (we suppose) Jesus taught no such doctrine – that alone might not be decisive – but because in addition no one in the relevant environment envisaged salvation in such modes or had such yearnings.

The experience of Jesus' impact was, then, both diverse and limited. I must repeat that it is also necessarily obscure. We lack sufficient information to tell the precise nature of the process whereby Jesus gave rise to particular kinds of experience; nor can we do more than form approximate ideas of experiences to which we give general terms like 'liberation' or 'reconciliation'. That there was something in his teaching or activity or career that gave rise to them is plain, but how the impact 'worked' to those ends we cannot know. Nor, of course, can we know why it 'worked' in certain cases and not in others. The nature of the 'meeting', the combination of two persons needed to produce the phenomenon here described, is not open to inspection. We can only say that it differed in character from case to case, and that in various ways it involved a contribution from both sides. It is even likely that this 'meeting' could involve what from outside might be described as misunderstanding, so that an observer of a particular instance might say, 'How could you experience the impact of Jesus in such a way that you see the régime of the Jewish Law, in this respect or that, as now at an end? – he meant no such thing.' Even so, the impact was made, the experience produced: that is the thing to be established. It is a fact that all such encounters involve a measure of movement which is capable of being described negatively as distortion ('he meant no such thing') or positively as active reception. He who makes impacts takes the risk of these twin verdicts – he casts his bread upon the waters. All the more so, if he does not put things in writing.[1] On the other hand, as far as our evidence goes, the impact of Jesus was not so utterly contradictory or diverse in its effects that we suspect sheer and blatant mistake of his intentions. Grave problems there certainly are in discovering, for example, his attitude to the Jewish Law – was it life-giving or death-dealing? – but we do not find the impact of Jesus being experienced as, let us say, both liberating and enslaving, blessing the rich in their riches as well as the poor in their poverty: it is quite consistent enough for us to use the general term 'salvation' and to mean by it new and deep well-being in relation to God, while at the same time acknowledging that such well-being varied considerably from person to person according to background and need.

The precise nature of the impact of Jesus is hidden from us, even though we certainly have enough information, refracted through the earliest church and the Gospels, to describe a number of its general features. And the experience to which it gave rise is accessible to us only indirectly and describable only in such wide terms as we have used – well-being, liberation, reconciliation. But we do have direct access to the third stage in the process whereby Christian theology came into being, that is, the *expression* of the experience in words, at any rate once they became written words. We may make intelligent guesses about the content of earlier oral expressions of Christian experience, in both Aramaic and Greek, but for hard information written words are our source, incomparably 'harder' than anything that preceded them. The articulation of experience in words is a crucial step. It involves both loss and gain.

Consider the nature of that step. It is not, of course, necessarily, perhaps not possibly, a step from wordlessness to wordness; rather, from the private to the public world and from fleetingness to the chance of permanence. Experience presents itself to us interiorly in verbal forms which are often fragmentary, ejaculatory, unrelated by logical structures or formal sentences; and intensity of conviction, generated by profound experience, is likely to increase these features, so that we may speak more readily of feelings and images than of words at all. But expression in outward verbal form involves a measure of conformity to a world of verbal conventions. It is a move from the family kitchen to the front parlour, a donning of Sunday clothes, and with it a loss of immediacy, naturalness, spontaneity, and even genuineness, all of them the price of greater communicability. It is, of course, possible to import into the outward verbal expression something of the intensity and spontaneity known interiorly. Then we speak of creativity in the speaker or writer: he has broken new ground, made old words do fresh work. Yet such creativity is limited by the demands of intelligibility. The expression of inner experience, felt as wholly novel, in wholly novel words, is a failure where communication is concerned.[12] It might as well not take place if anything other than the mere fact of the intensity of the experience is to be conveyed.

So, in the act of verbal expression, there is a loss of intensity and spontaneity, as also of the sheer personalness or privacy of the experience. But there is a gain in openness, accessibility and sharability. The gain is not wholly for those who are the readers or hearers of the words now produced. The writer or speaker may himself welcome a gain in clarity and coherence, the chance to dress his wares for a public. He may regret that he is failing to give an account of the intensity, and so of the reality, of what he knows to be true, but relieved to be able to put it into orderly words. There is a certain relaxation of pressure. Not just understanding but also responsibility is shared.

So it was when Paul first set out to convey Christian experience in written words. There is ample evidence of an intensity of experience bursting to express itself in new words, or even in no known words at all: the glossolalia he knew for himself as well as in others was perhaps of this character.[13] Expression in written words (as indeed already in orderly, spoken words) demanded discipline, conformity to conventional usage about meanings and even literary forms. There was room for creativity, that is, giving new meanings to old words under the demands of the new Christian subject-matter, but that creativity could bear only a limited measure of such adaptation – more would lead to unintelligibility. As it was, Paul went beyond those bounds as far as at least some of his readers were concerned: he was not understood, and at root, that meant that his experience was not theirs.[14]

Written expression also makes diversity of thought perfectly apparent. People may avow solidarity so long as what they are aware of is their common loyalty and only their own private experience of the object of that loyalty. They may even speak of that inner conviction but be so aware of their shared loyalty that the divergence in their ways of thinking about it is not apparent. Only written, orderly expression brings out that divergence and compels its recognition. It is likely, though not necessary, that such recognition will then lead to controversy, and so to the sharpening of opinions and perhaps to both the refinement and the distortion of previous expressions of experience. They are thereby removed further from the simplicity (maybe a confused simplicity) of the original experience. There is, then, what may be felt to be growth in orderly truthfulness; but from another point of view, there has been a movement away from a kind of raw truthfulness, so that what is said may be more rational, more defensible in argument, but less close to what is known in the heart.

Such a process is amply attested in the New Testament, as

we observe side by side the growing number of early Christian writers, wholly or partly independent of each other so far as we can see, though sometimes reacting to predecessors;[15] and all endeavouring to express in a range of literary forms their experience of the impact of Jesus.

It is probable that none of them experienced that impact directly in the ordinary historical sense. Even Paul's claim[16] to the parity of his experience of the risen Christ with that of apostolic and other predecessors does not refer to direct historical acquaintance with him. It is indeed in part an assertive attempt at compensation for the lack of such acquaintance. What difference does this indirectness make? It adds greatly to the usefulness of our examination of this first episode, or set of episodes, in the formation of Christian theology. It means that far removed from them as we are in time, we are in principle, in this respect, on precisely the same footing as they. For them as for us, the direct impact of Jesus was unknown, hidden behind the screen of other people's experience and oral (and perhaps written) verbal expression, or, putting it more positively, mediated through such experience and expression. We may properly refer to this first period and its testimony as 'pristine' and base its usefulness on its having that quality; but in this respect, its indirectness in relation to experience of Jesus, the pristine quality is marred. Yet in a way from which we can profit. We shall see shortly how that works.

There is a fourth stage in the formation of Christian theology, taking us beyond the verbal expression of experience by individuals or relatively simple and homogeneous groups as represented by individual writers. It is found already in the New Testament, even in embryo at a very early period,[17] but it is chiefly the work of later times. We may describe it as *formulation*. This is what occurs when the wider Christian body finds it desirable, for a variety of purposes, to agree on the written expression of its beliefs. The purpose may be protection against and refutation of what are seen as wrong beliefs, or it may be the provision of an agreed basis on which teaching may be given or allegiance expressed. It has, that is, a utilitarian purpose lacking, to this degree, in the process hitherto. True, any verbal expression takes place because it is in some way useful. But mere usefulness is not the motive; convenience is not uppermost. While the Gospel of Mark may have been written to provide a book for liturgical reading in the Marcan church or for the admonition of its members, and I Corinthians was written to correct certain errors in the congregation at Corinth, these works have a deeper purpose. They are born out of a concern with the Christian gospel – with the expression of Christian experience of Jesus in an appropriate form. But in the cases now in mind, church needs come to have the edge over other considerations.

These cases involve also, as a rule, an element of deliberate consensus, agreement between parties who, left to themselves, would put the matter differently, but for the common good accept the formula. Or else an element of official brevity: no individual would be content to express the matter so, for it would not do justice to experience, but the outward face of the community finds it desirable to offer a memorable official form of words to sum up its mind on an aspect of belief, or belief as a whole, thus made verbally manageable.[18]

Such formulation belongs at a greater distance from experience. If verbal expression involves, in relation to experience, entering the front parlour or donning the Sunday suit, formulation involves appearing on the public platform, bejewelled or bemedalled. There is a greater measure of artificiality or pose, an awareness of effect and a concern for political satisfactoriness.

It would be quite untrue to suggest that all these features are to be discerned in all cases. But the lineaments of some of them are present even in early cases of formulation like the summary of Christian proclamation in I Cor. 15.3f. Here Paul identifies himself with other Christians, even the Christian body as a whole. He uses terms which are not, perhaps, exactly his own most favoured way of expressing his faith, but to which he can nevertheless, for reasons of solidarity, give his allegiance.

But the more official the process of formulation becomes, the more the features outlined come to prominence.[19] The formulation may even represent what none of the parties involved actually believes for himself; that is, it may correspond to what none of them would willingly say in expressing their Christian experience for themselves. Nevertheless, in many circumstances, formulation may seem so important that these drawbacks fade into the background. Experience comes to be seen as largely private, perhaps dispensable, and certainly not as intimately linked to official statements of belief. 'Faith' is then less the direct response of the heart than adherence to formulas, seen as tests of loyalty, without a necessary close connection with experience or even (e.g. if the formulas are too technical for most people) the possibility of such connection. Experience there may be, but it will take its own private paths, and the public pressures will be in directions less and less related to it.

In such circumstances, the process we have been outlining for the formation of Christian theology is almost wholly reversed. Instead of experience of Christ yielding verbal expression which may lead on to official formulation in certain situations, we have the formulation as itself the measure and the fount of belief, which the individual may then feel he or she should translate into their own terms and use as the stimulus for personal inner experience. To describe this reverse process is not to decry it: clearly it has occurred in the lives of many faithful believers. But merely to describe it is to draw attention to its oddity. It involves using formulations of faith in a way that flies in the face of their own genesis and invites misunderstanding and complexity. For a person thus formed will easily conceive that Christian faith *is* adherence to the formulation, itself the oblique expression of other people's experience. He or she will then seek to 'know' God using those verbal tools, which were the outcome of a particular negotiation, perhaps long ago, and were designed for a purpose quite other than the use they are now made to serve. Formulation is then a perilous matter, engendering a feeling for belief as properly static and unyielding, embodied in talismanic forms of words whose virtue is chiefly felt to be in their status as symbols of group solidarity. Formulation accentuates a process which verbal expression already begins, but with a new range of effects, some of them seeming to vitiate the whole process of which this is the final stage. Its original purposes were inevitable, in some ways salutary, and certainly comprehensible in terms of the development of institutions, but its ultimate results are full of danger to the Christian's perception of faith, all the more for being so seductive and so useful to the church for many of its corporate ends.

The fourfold development of impact, experience, expression and formulation occurred haphazardly and by no uniform process in the early days of Christianity. Directly or indirectly, each of the stages is discernible in the New Testament writings and behind them. They appear there already in sufficiently complex form. 'Pristine' the New Testament examples may be, but only comparatively so. Already the stages criss-cross and interact with each other. Nevertheless, it is essential to grasp the fact and the nature of the process, for not only is it historically true but also it is full of thought-provoking instruction for the nature of Christian believing in later times.

I have already pointed to the distorting and even vitiating effect when the wrong role is given to the formulation of belief, and to the ease and frequency with which a wedge is thus driven between the official content of faith and personal experience. The effect is not, of course, by any means always to cause discontent – often quite the reverse. There is a sense of assurance, with settled faith secure in the hands of the competent authorities. Often, the effect is that Christians function at two levels, the credal and the personal, the didactic and the devotional, with a lack of contact between them, in idiom and frequently also in content. They have beliefs they rehearse and beliefs they live by.[20] In terms of the fourfold process, we may say that formulation is by no means always the appropriate instrument for the mediation of the impact of Jesus.

But there is a sense in which, even with the distorting effects produced by developments such as we have described, the fourfold process remains throughout Christian history the way in which, with infinite complexities, Christian articulation at all levels has come into being; and this is so, despite the fact that quite other models (e.g. the process of tradition) have been avowed and seem at first sight to give a better account of the matter. It is important to grasp this general applicability, for the fourfold process throws light on some aspects of current theological and religious difficulty: the widely felt disjunction between different levels of Christian discourse ('the pulpit' and 'the pew', or 'the theologian' and 'the simple believer'), and the frustrating disparity between official ecclesiastical pronouncements and 'grass-roots level' perception of the same issues. (There are here close links to the divergences of sensibility which we discussed earlier.) It offers hope of contributing to that formation of a realistic and unified theological outlook which is the major concern of this work.

But how are we to perceive the general applicability of this scheme? *Does* it throw light on reality? It has to be admitted that its bias is towards the individual believer as against the church. It can be seen to work more clearly in the life of the person than in that of the institution, and one might feel that in the long run it is institutions that count in the making of theology. Yet this is not to plead guilty to the charge of individualism; for though the identifiable location of religious faith is in persons, however much they may combine in churches, and though each person sees matters his own way and is responsible for his own belief, nevertheless individuals genuinely overlap in experience and understanding. Common belief and life are not the forced outcome of the interaction of total strangers.

Authentic Christian belief in any period has at its root, in some way or other, the impact of Jesus. The mode of the impact, now as always, back to the earliest examinable instances, is indirect. The mediating instrument may be as relatively simple as a reading of the Gospel of Mark or a hearing of stories about Jesus, or as complex as sophisticated credal formulas about him, results of an earlier instance of the fourfold process. It may be the reception of Holy Communion or sharing in the life of a Christian group, recognized as vehicles of Jesus; or, more obliquely, by way of music or painting, or almost any kind of beneficent act or impulse seen as conveying him.

The phrase 'impact of Jesus' needs qualifying in two ways. First, Christian belief has its root in *what is perceived as* the impact of Jesus. The genuineness is far from guaranteeable; a degree of inadequacy and inaccuracy is in all cases undeniable. Nevertheless, we may speak of the impact of Jesus, if only because no other starting-point is at all appropriate. The misleadingness (to a greater or lesser degree) of what is perceived as 'Jesus' is an instance of the inevitable condition involved in receiving the impact of any historical figure whatsoever, even when the evidence is a great deal more abundant than in the case of Jesus. It is indeed a necessary feature of the relationship between persons, even contemporaries and intimates.

Second, Christian belief is rooted in the impact of Jesus seen as himself the one from God and the mediator of relationship with him. In other words, it is a Jesus who is seen, at least in a general sense, christologically. There is, however, for our purposes no call to specify that christology further, no need to guard against 'errors' or to fill out the picture – only to specify the *fact* of christology and to put the matter of Jesus in a theistic context: Jesus as the one from God. Without such a context, the impact of Jesus is not a religious or theological matter at all, simply a matter of his making an impression as of one human figure on another, demanding no wider interpretation.

For that impact to have effect, in the process of leading to belief, there must be at some stage what can be identified as need or as the experience of salvation; that is, some kind of acceptable and intelligible well-being in relation to God (and so to a person's or a group's whole world). Plainly, it is not necessary in practice that these elements should be overt from the start, as in the case of those initiated into Christianity from infancy and reared in an environment of faith; or that they should be perceived at the time as receiving what may be describable as the impact of Jesus. The impact may (it has always been so) itself awaken the need and fashion the shape of the experience, which should then develop in depth and character.

The verbal expression is the most obvious point at which the complexity of the process is apparent. Few Christian believers will, except in special circumstances, bring forth their own original expressions of experience, even perhaps in their private prayers. Especially if they are 'well instructed' believers, acquainted with scripture and other Christian literature, they will turn to existing verbal expressions which, with no doubt varying degrees of adequacy, 'hit off' their experience and indeed then go on to form it anew. So what is not initially their own, they make their own. In societies like ours, where the material of Christian culture and the educational means for its transmission are not readily available or have become unfashionable, there will be a decline in the number of those making their own the expressions of earlier Christian experience;[21] and some will feel compelled to provide their own new modes of expression, whether in prayer or in affirmations of belief. In this there is loss and gain: the loss of the 'riches of the past' (and for that matter the dross of the past too!), with their evocative and formative quality, but a gain in immediacy to experience and so in authenticity. There is a price to pay in shallowness – and a greater responsibility put on believers to discover in themselves the thoughts and words which satisfactorily give account of their experience and understanding. There is less external verbal support on which to lean than in the past,[22] and depth is often found instead in the more open sharing of experience with fellow-believers.

The verbal expression of faith exists at many levels of sophistication and competence; each instance has its place and may make its way – from a popular hymn or a halting contribution to a parish discussion-group to a learned article or lecture. As never before, each may feel itself possessed of validity and a right to exist. No wonder such a revolution brings alarm, not only at the loss of authority, but also at the apparent squandering of a whole heritage of discrimination in the expression of Christian experience – partly at the hands of the organs of authority themselves.[23]

Formulation remains at some distance from Christian experience, and its uses remain as they have always been: the public and official purposes of the wider church. They are removed from the more personal purposes for which people come to believe and for which they continue in devotion and Christian life. This element still carries public weight and esteem, even among believers who make scant use of it.[24]

The understanding of the process by which Christian theology comes into being is, then, the second major contribution which a consideration of New Testament studies can offer to the building up of a unified theological outlook. It can give not only understanding but also hope of what is to be achieved and a sight of the responsibility falling upon the believer within the complex life of the Christian community in society. To see the doctrinal task, in any period or setting, as essentially not the handing on and interpreting of the tradition, but the working out once more of the fourfold scheme, is above all to experience an accession of confidence. It urges upon each fresh group or individual a frank appraisal of *experience* and a will to be faithful to it. It encourages realism in the *expression* of experience, and a certain mistrust of *formulation* through a recognition of its limited usefulness. And it refuses to allow awareness of the *impact* of Jesus to be lost in the welter of other interests and concerns which the Christian thinker inevitably encounters, just as it also fosters alertness to the dangers of that impact being blunted by travesties in the presentation of Jesus.

In this perspective, each new attempt at the doctrinal task has its own independent validity – and responsibility. It cannot commend itself simply by leaning on the past or be determined by what was once authentic and once answered to the needs of the times. In this perspective, each new attempt is in the same position as the first Christian writers whose work we see in the New Testament. We all, of whatever age, stand in a circle, looking inwards to the common centre on which we depend, Jesus and all he gives; and though we may rightly look along to others in the circle and derive great good, each has his own charge which no one else can take off his shoulders.

Study of the New Testament promotes other reflections which are to do more purely with the content of belief. If one thing is increasingly plain as a result of modern study of the New Testament, it is that the distinctiveness of Christianity in its beginnings within its Jewish setting lay primarily, if not exclusively, in its relation to the figure of Jesus. In formal terms, christology was its only really new and substantial doctrine. It was its central and determinative concern, the spring from which the rest of its newness flowed.

This may seem to be the merest truism, but in certain important ways it is far from being anything of the sort. It points to a particular way of looking at Christian doctrine as a whole. Traditional and customary accounts of that doctrine see it as taking its rise *de novo* with the life, death and resurrection of Jesus, and as a self-contained body of teachings which are both distinguishable from each other and mutually coherent. Yet, though, as we have shown, it is proper and intelligible to see the formation of Christian theology from the start as beginning with the impact of Jesus, nevertheless the understanding of Jesus can only err if it fails to take full account of his setting in Judaism. And what is true of Jesus is true of his first followers,

including those whose written work is available to us in the
New Testament. Every one of them possessed a mind formed in
Jewish faith, holding one or another of the patterns of belief
based on the scriptures which were current at the time. These
patterns included beliefs about God and his mode of communication with man, about God's purposes for his people and the
nature of his relationship with them as with mankind in
general. In the case of 'the Christian phenomenon', if, for the
moment, belief be thought of as a set of items, then the only
extra item is constituted by 'Jesus'. And while particular
writers attend more to one side or another of his work, across
their whole range it is a matter of both Jesus as the preacher of a
message and Jesus as himself the subject of others' preaching.
Whether as, in his lifetime, the proclaimer or, after it, as the
proclaimed one, 'Jesus' is *the* new element in belief. From this
point of view, it is misleading to say that Jesus as the subject of
beliefs or doctrines is to be distinguished from Jesus as the
first-century Galilean preacher and healer. Both fuse together
in the Jesus who is believed in, whose impact is received.

Such a way of putting it is both true and also inadequate. For
while, in formal terms, the 'Jesus phenomenon' was no more
than an extra item in already existing patterns of belief (and
Christians commit absurdities in forgetting that), still for them
it had a transforming effect on the existing Jewish patterns of
belief. Even beliefs which in a formal sense remained the same
and required no alteration (e.g. beliefs about God as creator),
in another sense acquired a wholly new character; for 'Jesus'
coloured them afresh. We may not unfairly describe the work of
Paul as crucial just because it was one of the most thorough-
going agencies by which it was shown how 'Jesus' transmuted
all existing areas of belief – or (it is almost jargon) transformed Paul's 'world' (and, according to his conviction about it,
everybody's world). It has become increasingly evident[25] that
it was the colouring of his beliefs by 'Jesus' which was the sole
significant novelty in his belief as he turned Christian. Other
major aspects of his theological thought, such as justification by

faith, the community of believers seen as Christ's 'body' or 'bride', or life in the Spirit, were children of this fundamental new feature, not independently generated items in a catalogue of newly acquired beliefs. They were some of the implications for his already existing faith of his new conviction that Jesus was the one from God, his agent for the fulfilment of his age-old saving purpose for his people and indeed for mankind. In other words, Paul's ideas were not his ways of solving a series of theological problems or even personal problems (e.g. How may I be saved? How may man get right with God?), but the results of reflection on the sheer generosity of God in the coming of Jesus. In the light of that gift, nothing could remain unaffected, and from the start the task of Christian theology was to consider how its results were to be understood in the light of existing belief.

With the completion of the career of Jesus, and so the end of the period of his preaching, we may begin to speak of the articulating of his impact in terms of more formal christology; that is, doctrines about him in the light of God. But it follows from what has been said that it is misleading to use that term if it is taken to mean one topic of belief and articulation in a series of beliefs, or one formal intellectual construction alongside others. It is true that it has often taken these forms and been discussed in these terms, but they do less than justice to the facts of the matter; for the doctrines derive from and depend on that which lies deeper, simply the receiving of the impact of Christ within the believer's personal setting. Moreover, christology is not a department of belief or understanding to be worked out and then put by, as one turns one's mind to other sides of belief; rather it is, for the Christian, the determinative centre for belief as a whole. In this way, the New Testament suggests a particular proportioning of belief and a particular mode of seeing it as a single style of perception.

We noticed the common distinction between Jesus as a historical figure and Jesus as a belief-laden figure. We shall now attend to this distinction, before following a further line of reflection derived from the study of the New Testament.

The two ways of regarding Jesus are distinguishable in the New Testament and so, it seems, in the experience of the Christian movement in its first decades. Of course the Gospels, which present Jesus ostensibly as a figure of history, are themselves 'belief-laden' in their approach to him, but implicit in the very enterprise of writing them is interest in him as a man whose story can be told. The story is told in theologically determined modes of expression (e.g. as affected by Old Testament prophecy and so by a view of history and of human existence as divinely directed), but it is nevertheless narrative in form and a presentation of Jesus as having identifiable characteristics: however many the obscurities, it is plain that he stands for certain causes rather than others, even plainer that certain ways of assessing him (e.g. as tyrannical, as a political agitator, a tool of the rich, or a meticulous rabbinic casuist) are to be excluded. By contrast, Paul, on the testimony of his letters, presents a Jesus who is virtually without such characteristics: he is one who is *acted upon* (above all by God), rather than one who *acts*. Chiefly, he is put to death and raised. In such a perspective, the emphasis edges towards propositional belief rather than narrative that appeals to the imagination and the heart, on Jesus as a kind of doctrinal symbol rather than a person whose story elicits vivid personal response.[26]

Here, at the very start of Christianity, we may see the roots of two kinds of christology whose fortunes have ebbed and flowed in various periods and at various levels of Christian life. Jesus as the doctrinal symbol is the subject of the classical christological controversies and definitions and of the more recent christological discussions and proposals which, while challenging the classical doctrinal patterns, have followed their lead in this crucial respect. They often seem to work in terms of a Jesus who is scarcely recognizable to the historically and personally minded. They take as given *a priori* ideas about Jesus, for example that he was sinless, which are impossible to substanti-

ate historically and very difficult even to comprehend, once the
element of relativity in what constitutes 'sin' and the processes
of human psychological formation are recognized. (By most
standards of charitable discourse, would not a Jesus who
uttered the words of Matt. 23 be open to moral censure? Of
course those words may not be authentic, but that is another
matter.)

Jesus as the person with a story has reappeared in the various
manifestations of 'Jesus piety' which have flowered in many
forms in Christian history, outwardly expressed chiefly in
painting, sculpture, poetry and music, and nourishing Christian devotion at every level, as well as in the more austere and
objective investigations of 'the Jesus of history' in recent times.

Now, however influential and large-scale the sense of the
Jesus of story has been, it is clear that, in official esteem, 'hard
truth' has been reckoned to be available almost exclusively in
the former, more conceptual stream. The latter stream has
been, in this evaluation, secondary, representing a 'softer', less
fundamental and reliable kind of truth. Indeed, so dominant
has the former stream been, that in the pre-critical era even the
manifestations of Jesus piety were overshadowed by it within
their own being; so that it was less a question of devotion to
Jesus 'as he really was' than to the divine humanity of the
saviour, a figure in whom story was the servant of concept even
when 'story' was the mode of discourse or of representation. It
is certainly a 'doctrine-laden' Jesus, not a historical Jesus as we
now conceive the matter, who moves the listener to J. S. Bach's
St Matthew Passion or the reader of *Jesu, dulcis memoria* or *Stabat
mater dolorosa*.[27]

It is an important role of New Testament studies to suggest
that this evaluation be reconsidered. We can ask for frank
recognition of the cultural factors affecting Paul and his many
successors in the former stream of the Christian tradition,
which have led to its dominance as a way of regarding belief
concerning Jesus. It arose not because it was the only possible
way of expressing Christian belief – that is belied by the

existence of the alternative tradition, with the Gospels at its
head; or because it has some kind of absolute claim to
'correctness' or usefulness – manifestly, its abstract character
itself removes it largely from the sphere of ordinary experience
and makes it more accessible to intellectuals and officers in the
church than to the great majority; but because it was fostered
by the prevalence of certain conceptual patterns in the
Christian environment and by politico-ecclesiastical forces to
whom its relative neatness was useful and congenial. But once
accord the alternative tradition a hearing in its own right, and a
different perspective opens up on both the manner and the
content of belief.

It is not simply a matter of the by now fairly familiar point
that each of the Gospels has its own distinctive theological
outlook, so that we are encouraged, by that very fact, to
recognize the legitimacy and the potentiality of theological
diversity.[28] Nor is it just that their narrative character stimulates us to think theologically in less abstract terms and to be
less afraid to give rein to the heart and the imagination in
forming our theological outlook and making Christian judgments. There is another aspect of the business of arriving at
theology and belief, again put before us in pristine form in the
Gospels.

Those writings are not simply narratives, four tellings of the
story of Jesus, or presentations of Jesus by way of narrative.
Each of them is in fact the fruit of the intertwining of two
'stories' or streams of experience, that of Jesus himself and that
of the evangelist.[29] The former has its objectivity but is only
accessible to us by way of the latter. By the evangelist's story we
mean his total experience, all that has gone to 'make' him, up to
the moment of his writing. Thus it includes his genetic and
cultural inheritance and his interaction with the particular
Christian circle for which, no doubt, he acts as spokesman. It is
important to recognize that this intertwining of stories is the
necessary condition of the forming not only of these but of all
expressions of belief. So it applies not just to those that emerge

in obviously story form, but also to those that appear in conceptual form, even those that seem most rigidly abstract, propositional or impersonal. It is plain that Paul's conceptual mode of expression is the vehicle for an interaction of his story with that of Jesus. It is less plain in the case of the deliverances of a council in creed, articles and anathemas or the work of academic writers who are deliberately detached from the immediacies of church life and who seek to transcend the impulses of prejudice and fashion; but it is true also of them. In all cases (including the present writer), it is, we now recognize perhaps more vividly than ever, possible and illuminating to ask: What is the 'story' of those who write and speak? What in their experience leads them to think as they do? Can we discern how and why their particular emphases arise? The aim of this kind of interrogation is not to discredit those subjected to it, though inevitably and rightly it counteracts the tendency to give absolute and definitive value to any particular formulation of belief, any single interaction of a Christian's story with the story of Jesus. That is in itself of the greatest importance – and we arrive once more, by another route, at the style of awareness we have reached before in this book: Christian theological statement is not to be seen, if we take seriously the conditions of its formation as revealed by modern theological study, as 'definition'. However august the authority by whom it is stated, it is always the fruit of the intertwining of stories, the adoption of one possibility among others. The interrogation then promotes realism, self-awareness in believing, and a certain style of responsible freedom.

It is, of course, open to organs of authority, for the promotion of order and the avoidance of confusion (where those are regarded as great goods), to lay particular beliefs or styles of theological statement upon their members. But we now know that such action neither enhances nor diminishes their claim to rational acceptance. It belongs in the realm of discipline, not in the realm of truth-telling. However careful and profound the statements in question, however deserving of respect, their limited character is plain to see. On the other hand, it is no part of this argument to suggest that theological statements are, because of this limited and subjective character, all equally commendable or that belief should be a free-for-all. The realization that belief reaches expression by the intertwining of stories and should be evaluated as such is a spur to carefulness of theological reflection upon experience: it is important that the believer esteem and evaluate his or her story with a candour and serious honesty which makes it no mockery for it to intertwine with the story of Jesus. It lays upon him or her a salutary responsibility far greater than that often conveyed by more clear-cut ways of exercising authority, which easily remain external in their effects.

The realization which this line of thought produces has the additional value of not just prompting the exploiting of experience (the believer's story) but also counteracting it, as a result of fuller and more candid awareness. Thus, there is little doubt that the classical expressions of Christian belief, emphasizing the triumph of Christ and his cosmic lordship, derived not only from a train of logical development going back to the resurrection and ascension, but also from the euphoria produced by the ascendancy of Christianity in the Roman Empire from the time of Constantine.[30] The church was very pleased to be at last in a position of worldly power, and doctrine conformed readily. There is equally little doubt that this development led to the playing-down of other aspects of Christian sensibility which stare one in the face in the story of Jesus: his identification with the outcast, the stress on powerlessness, and the centrality of suffering and self-denial. It is evident that, through lack of self-criticism, the intertwining of the two stories was defective in its thoroughness – in this case (it is no exaggeration to say) with catastrophic consequences for the church's self-awareness in relation to society, perhaps even more than for theology itself.

Again, a person whose life is marked by deprivation and rejection may identify almost wholly, in interacting with the story of Jesus, with corresponding elements in that story, above all with the crucifixion. Those who rest there may fail to perceive the possibilities of hope and to be alert to God in the light of them; but then they will be failing to allow the story of Jesus to interact fully with their own. Likewise, priests with responsibility for mission to the utterly poor and powerless may be led to similar identification with the humanly negative aspects in the story of Jesus and to consequent rejection of the present structures of society. In such cases, church authorities are inclined to appeal to the propositional, doctrinal tradition in order to bring about a more balanced reaction; and then there is a clash of theologies both in method and in content. It may be more constructive if the story of Jesus, with which interaction is sought, is approached with greater historical realism, such as modern study is well placed to provide. In that case, over-easy identification will be avoided, additional features in Jesus' theological background (e.g. concerning creation and eschatology) will come to awareness, and wiser (which does not mean less radical) theological judgments will emerge; moreover, they will emerge not by externally imposed *fiat* but through a more adequate involvement of those concerned with the Jesus whose story is for them theologically and personally creative.

It seems inevitable that a person exposed first to the more conceptual tradition, with its expression in propositional theological tenets, and then to the 'story' approach which emerges from taking seriously the Gospels in particular, will be confronted with two distinct sets of beliefs: the authorized and agreed set of beliefs of the church to which he or she belongs and the beliefs by which he or she lives and which have been adopted as a result of experience (that is, letting the stories intertwine). It is not uncommon to find that people willing to embrace the former find it impossible to give many of them meaning in life or to see means whereby they can affect outlook and behaviour. In our terms, the reason is the simple one that, for them, the beliefs have not emerged from any genuine interaction of their story with the story of Jesus and its implications. That in turn may be because of insufficient effort of mind and imagination to see where such interaction can be discerned, or to turn technical theological categories into more usable terms – in effect relating the two sets of beliefs to each other. But it may be that the conceptual beliefs were simply ideas that have died or become outmoded, so that no such translation can avail. It can be more tragic when conceptual beliefs stemming purely from external authority are seen as the only possibility; then, when they are found unusable, a person's story proceeds without any effective influence from Christian belief, for want of any point of attachment. Such a situation can perfectly well co-exist with the avowal of fervent attachment to the official agenda of beliefs. They then function simply as a banner or rallying-point.

Before ending this chapter, I turn to one more example of the ways in which modern study of the New Testament can have far-reaching effects on doctrinal thinking, even to the extent of setting puzzling doctrinal problems in a wholly new light and perhaps showing them up as mirages. In this case, the aspect of New Testament study involved is one that has come to the fore in recent years – the application to the situations represented in the New Testament of perspectives drawn from sociology. It is in effect yet one more refinement of the acute historical awareness which has dominated New Testament studies in the modern period.[31]

It is evident that any human group inherits or constructs for itself a 'symbolic universe' – a mode of understanding the world in terms of which it finds identity and security and which it comes to see as axiomatic. Such a symbolic universe or, in its religious aspect, 'sacred canopy' is bound, for the sake of comprehensiveness, to involve a way of understanding the present in the light of both past and future. Such an embedding of the present in a total time-sequence is indeed a powerful agent of security and worth inventive effort, even if the facts of history do not readily lend themselves to it. So nations live with versions of their past which remember victories and erase defeats. So English constitutional reformers, rejecting the excesses of the Stuart monarchy in the seventeenth century, appealed to mythical Anglo-Saxon liberties which the 'Norman yoke', perpetuated by subsequent royal rulers, had suppressed. So too modern liturgical reformers commend their productions the more effectively by claiming to restore the shape of the eucharist in the early church, disregarding the numerous differences of ethos, language and style between early church worship and that of today.[32] So, finally, modern charismatic Christians, who might be expected to rest content with the present spontaneous authority of the Spirit, appeal to the activities described in I Corinthians 14, regardless of the fact that the whole drift of Paul's argument in that chapter is to damp them down.

The early church, deriving from the impact of Jesus, who thus gave it its 'present', was no exception to the need to support its sense of identity by framing a full-blown symbolic universe: it needed a past and a future. The former could plausibly come only from 'Israel', that is, from the Jews seen as God's people in the terms laid out in many literary forms in their scriptures. It is therefore no surprise that almost every early Christian writer wrestles with (or at least deals with) this issue in one form or another: how did Jesus (the present, as far as Christians were concerned) stand in relation to Judaism (representing the past)? How did the church stand in relation to Israel as a community, the old scriptures as a body of theological writings, and Judaism as a religion? As is well known, there was no single, agreed way of answering those questions. Between them, those writers represent almost every possible view, short of the two extremes of outright rejection and pure continuity – and even those answers were in fact given by other Christians whose points of view find no clear voice in the canonical writings.[33] Moreover, it is no exaggeration to say that the church has never been able to decide on a single, fully coherent answer to those questions, but has lived with a combination of ideas ranging from a sense of the fulfilment in Christ of God's beneficent work in the old Israel to fierce antisemitism; from an insistence on Christianity's 'special relationship' with Judaism, both historically and theologically, to a rejection of its religious worth – with different aspects coming to the fore in different periods and circumstances. Yet, as Christian thinkers, from Paul onwards, have agonized over these questions, it has been in terms of a view of them as theological problems to which solutions should, given adequate insight, be available. We may *now* see them as vital elements in a quest for identity which, in the nature of the circumstances, admitted of no single response. In order to establish themselves, Christians were bound to adopt both positive and negative attitudes towards the parent body and to veer from the one to the other. Further, they were bound to confuse the question of relating to what was, factually, their background (i.e. Judaism) with the question of establishing a theological understanding of God's purposes (expressed in Israel, then Christ and the church derived from him).

If it was inevitable that Christians sought a past in Israel, it was equally inevitable that they initially sought a future by appropriating the conventions of Jewish apocalyptic. It was by far the readiest option available to them in their setting. It was assimilated to their present (Jesus) by placing him at the centre of the apocalyptic picture which they adopted: he would be, indeed already was (so thoroughly was future welded on to present), the agent of the fulfilment of God's purposes for the universe, would return, and would reign in triumph.[34] Thus, assurance and stability were amply provided, with Jesus as their content and guarantor. The panoramic view of time, already begun by 'Israel', was completed by 'knowledge' of the programme of events leading to the End.

But of course, just as the questions about relations with Israel did not admit of, and certainly did not receive, a clear and single answer, so the beliefs about the future suffered from an even more devastating weakness: they were never fulfilled. More and more, they faded from view, were postponed to a continually shifting time ahead, or were transmuted into new beliefs about life after death, heaven and hell, and eventually the whole mediaeval apparatus of purgatory with its intimate links to religious life in this world. It is then the case that both vital elements in the first Christians' symbolic universe are wholly problematic. While both undoubtedly served their purpose, both are a tangle of confused notions and unsatisfactory answers. A sociological approach to their beginnings in the New Testament may yield a different perspective.

Let us make a rigorous attempt to see early Christian attitudes to their relationship with God's Israel (exemplified in Paul's agonized argument in Romans 9–11) and early Christian ideas about a future catastrophe initiated by God (exemplified in Mark 13 and the Apocalypse of John) in sociological terms, as a prelude to re-evaluating briefly their theological significance. They were the ways in which those Christians, working in their setting (in terms of their 'stories'), sought identity and intelligibility for themselves. In truth, all they really knew and had, at the factual level, was 'Jesus' – whose impact was the basis of their distinctive experience and institutional existence as a community; and all they knew and had that was distinctive at the theological level was belief about him in the light of their already existing belief in God. Both the ideas about Israel and those about the End which were so quickly generated were then wholly conditioned by time and circumstance. They were not 'hard' doctrine, but simply attempts to solve pressing problems in the only terms then available. And, as far as 'Israel' was concerned, there was a fatal confusion between what was of course the case as a matter of historical cause and effect, and theological necessity.

Is there not then freedom for other Christians, receiving the impact of Jesus in their own time and place, to form their own identity by seeing past and future, and indeed the wider present, in terms drawn naturally from present circumstances?

And would not such a release transform, among other things, Jewish-Christian relations, attitudes to other faiths and, for some, attitudes to the future, all of which have so frequently been hamstrung by attempts to remain somehow faithful to New Testament ideas, seen as 'hard' doctrine, or guilt at neglecting them because they were found unusable?

It may be contested whether such interactions as those we have described show promise of anything as full-blooded as that satisfactory, unified theological and religious outlook which is our hope and goal in this book. Such an outlook is never, of course, a finished product: it evolves and develops as the interacting self (and the interacting Christian community in its various expressions) evolves and develops in time and space. Its adequacy in a particular case depends largely on the depth of reflection and the range of considerations which are brought to the task: to sow little is to reap little.

If adequacy depends on such ill-defined factors as depth of reflection and the width of the range of considerations brought into play, is there not a risk of intolerable diversity of judgment and pattern in theological and religious outlooks to be found within supposedly unified communities? I can only repeat, first, that such diversity is a constant feature of Christian history once its realities are uncovered and official pronouncements of what is to be believed are not taken to have a monopoly of esteem or to be effective in the way that has often been assumed; second, that it is habit that makes the diversity 'intolerable', and we need a change of mind at this crucial point – encouraged by some of the reflections prompted by taking New Testament studies seriously; and third, that it is more a question of maturity than of anarchic wildness. There has to be trust that believers, who have the responsibility of 'working out' their faith along the lines suggested and have received the necessary tools, will do it with genuine and thorough reflection; and in such circumstances there is a large area of consensus, freely reached. Of course there is the risk that false tracks will be followed: paths of valid development in belief cannot be foreseen, and validity itself in these matters can only arise in the end from trust in the wisdom of those who engage in the task with all the devotion, honesty and comprehensiveness that can be mustered. Theological and religious judgment is comparable to the taste acquired by the connoisseur of an art, a craft or a wine. There is room for the acquiring of ample knowledge and the unceasing pursuit of excellence in the art which is the object of love; but there is always room too for diversity of judgment and of esteem. This is supremely true in the subtle and complex matter of man's relationship with God within a long and rich tradition of faith, enquiry and devotion.

The starting-point I have chosen, in New Testament studies, has its limitations. It does not easily lead to integration with certain important and problematic areas of Christian thought, notably those most naturally analysed with the use of philosophical tools: the objectivity of God's existence, how to conceive of his action in the world, and how to justify his ways to man. In other words, from some points of view the way taken here starts some way down the path of enquiry. The contribution of those who 'listen to' modern New Testament studies lies chiefly in their refined historical awareness and in their insistent questions to other theological disciplines arising from that awareness. Those taking that discipline as their starting-point and as the context of religious commitment and theological thought can only work with that awareness to the fore.

The analysis and, still more, the remedies adopted in this book will fail to appeal to many whose starting point is different. Some will hold that New Testament studies, historically pursued, are no place to begin theological enquiry: it needs a philosophical grounding or an elucidating of God's ways and of his revelation, taken as 'given'. In other words, we can do no *theological* good without taking a conceptual path. It will be clear that this book has no wish to deny other starting-points their place – on the contrary, it welcomes them. And, from one point of view, the highest claim it makes for New Testament studies in relation to theology as a whole is that they must not be gainsaid. What they tell of truth is simply *there*: they are not rocks to be circumnavigated, but lands to be lingered in and tended. They are territory in which *Christian* theology, whatever its starting-point, must learn to be thoroughly at home.

Again, those for whom Christian doctrine is seen as a traditional, defined body of beliefs to be inherited, explored and restated will find much that is uncongenial. They have been given some questions which require an answer. Others, who claim spirituality as the place where the integration of theological study and religious commitment should take place, must think carefully before they find the approach taken here unhelpful. They are, it is true, being invited implicitly to question ideas and practices they may hold dear: that is a risk which those who seek God should be ready to run. More deeply, they are asked to consider a brand of ascesis which makes hard demands on mind and heart. It may be none the worse for that. The next chapter considers some aspects of this side of our subject.

-6-

New Testament Study and the Religious Quest

It is idle to hope to take important steps towards the reconstruction envisaged here and to remain unscathed. If areas of knowledge and experience that have been insulated from each other are brought together, then there is almost bound to be friction and pain, above all where treasured practices and deeply held beliefs are called in question.

Modern New Testament study has done more to occasion such friction than any other branch of theological work. It has both set in a new and problematic light many parts of the traditional patterns of belief and, for many, it has made the New Testament no longer usable in ways long established in Christian devotion. It is no wonder that people often steer clear of such study; no wonder that some who are exposed to it seem determined, perhaps intuitively, to hold it at arm's length and to keep it from encroaching on the more intimate aspects of Christian allegiance. This book is written in the belief that such segregation is stultifying and inhibits growth. However intractable they may appear to be from the viewpoint of the 'inner self', areas of truth which that self has no reasonable grounds for rejecting cannot healthily be locked away in a chamber of the mind, as if in quarantine, perhaps receiving occasional visits but prevented from any substantial part in the development of that self. The fear is, of course, that if let loose they will

94

wreak havoc in everything around. Sometimes it is hoped that such risk can be avoided by following moderate policies: it is not New Testament study in itself, even in its modern forms, that causes difficulty, but only its more radical conclusions; and they are matters of opinion, not yet assured results. Such easy hope is not justified. As we have seen, it is the very methods of New Testament study that cause us to think out our whole position afresh, with their rigorous historical demands and the light in which they set Christian origins. Anyway, those radical conclusions are certainly on the scene, and whether accepted or not, are within the range of legitimate opinion.

So there is fear that unmanageable truth will get loose. We have seen something of the effects of such release on ways of thinking about Christian belief, and in the second part of this book other, more specific examples will be worked out. It is inevitable that traditional ways of believing should demand revision, and even central aspects of the content of belief need reappraisal. For that reason, the fear is not misplaced; but, once more, Christian faith carries with it no guarantee that human ways of thinking about it and about its traditional tenets are beyond such revision. It is ironical that increased historical awareness has had two quite contrary effects. To some has come the liberating recognition of the sheer scale of such revision in the past: formerly, through lack of historical awareness, it generally took place unconsciously and indeed in the name of faithfulness to tradition.[1] But to others study of the past has brought the possibility of a clearer picture of that to which they are determined to adhere.[2] Both reappraisal and traditionalism now have the means to be more efficient than ever before. If the challenge to traditional modes of believing is now acute, it is largely a measure of the revolution that has occurred in the study of the New Testament, as in so many areas of enquiry, and of the common reluctance to absorb its effects. It is a measure of the contrast, no longer so capable of disguise or mitigation as in former times,[3] between traditional ways of using scripture and aspects of truth about it which are, with all their angularity and with all the difficulty involved in assimilating them, now simply *there* before us.

We have not so far gone beyond general principles in discussing the implications of taking New Testament studies seriously for that even more sensitive area, the expression of religious commitment. A specific example will now throw them into relief. It could scarcely be more germane to our central concerns.

There is a yawning gulf of tone and ethos between modern linguistic and historical study of the Gospels and traditional ways of using them meditatively. It is a prime instance of the contrasting styles of sensibility which we described earlier. The former is rigorously analytical; the latter simply *receives* the text as offered to the mind and imagination, in a manner that is naive from the point of view of historical criticism, though it may be rich in traditional technicalities of its own. What the former takes as evidence to be interrogated as to its historical or literary status, the latter accepts as unproblematic data for religious apprehension. It has no inclination even to raise the issue of historical value and feels resentment, a threat of spiritual vandalism, if that issue is raised in its presence. The meditative use may be described, perhaps disparagingly, as 'pre-critical', but that description does not do justice to its continuing vitality in devotional life and its capacity to give the benefits of immediacy between reader and text. It brings out the affinity and continuity which undoubtedly exists between the ancient writer and the modern reader and which is played down by the emphasis on discontinuity inherent in historical study. The sense of continuity or immediacy may occur in any reading of an ancient text, for those who find it still attractive or intelligible despite the distance of time and culture; in the case of the use of the New Testament in Christian meditation, there is the extra factor of common, strong directedness towards the figure of Jesus and towards God through him. Still, there is no doubt that many, who are initially intent both on study of the Gospels, using the tools now available, and on having them play a part in prayer, find their situation intolerable, as the fruits of study obtrude inappropriately into prayer and as the attitudes of devotion make study seem futile, trivial and irreligious. Again, it is no wonder that one occupation or the other is given up in what seems like inevitable defeat.

But supposing a person is intent on taking the study of the Gospels seriously and also concerned that the figure of Jesus portrayed in them should play a part in his deliberate reflection in the presence of God, then considerations like these may be held in mind.

1. It is possible that the radical solution is right. One occupation or the other has to go, for they are indeed incompatible. The traditional meditative use of the Gospels is part and parcel of an approach to the Gospels which, in other contexts, has simply been discarded. It is a survival. No one now involved in the serious study of the Gospels reads them naively, as if we can discern Jesus directly within their pages; not even conservative scholars do. If we are able to discern him at all, it has to be through and behind those pages. In that case, with whatever regrets, the honest person must jettison this way of using the Gospels in prayer. 'Jesus' can no longer be encountered along this path. What is there encountered is not the Jesus of historical reality, but a presentation of him which has been subjected to many kinds of influence. Meditation of the traditional kind on the Gospels has simply had its day. It is, after all, at least in its familiar and more formalized modes, the product of a particular period in Christian history, chiefly Catholic Christianity of the sixteenth and seventeenth centuries, and however greatly it has won favour it cannot count on perpetual life.[4] Anyway, the loss is not crippling. It is just that one technique of prayer, which always lent itself to fantasy, is found wanting. There is no challenge to meditative prayer itself, only to one method which turns out to be flawed. We now see that it did not achieve what it seemed to achieve, identification with the historical figure of Jesus.

2. We come to a similar conclusion if we test the value of

another defence often used for the direct religious use of the Gospels: even if they are to be interpreted for academic purposes by means of the techniques of scholarship, their divine authority or inspiration may still be understood to transcend the findings of scholarship and sanction their direct use in meditative prayer. There is still truth and reality in seeing scripture as a text on the page before us,[5] as a vehicle of communication from God to man.[6] In fact, however, this defence will not do the work required of it. However high our doctrine of the authority or inspiration of scripture, it does nothing to alleviate the situation. In no way can it do away with the obstinately historical nature of these texts, as of all texts; a realization which, once gained, cannot by any means be wished away. It is part of the inescapable truth about them. The questions posed to the traditional ways of devotion related to the Gospels will not accept dismissal on these grounds.

3. We can, however, make the stronger claim that texts are susceptible of different kinds of enquiry and use, without our falling into unhealthy compartmentalizing of ourselves or disparaging one use in order to favour another. It is a question of the different significances which a text can properly bear for different readers or even the same reader in different situations. If our aim is to 'listen to' the evangelist, then we must recognize that though he had *a meaning* which we should do our utmost to recover, there is no reason (and certainly no chance) that his effect should be so limited. Every hearer contributes willy-nilly to his sense of what is heard; significances spread like ripples and diversify as they spread.[7] There is no obscurantism in all this, no rejection of the fruits of study or of the rigour with which it declines to indulge mere wilful and lazy subjectivity. The process is held in check by its own self-consciousness; the interpreter, range though he will, knows what he is doing and observes himself in the act. There is no reason in principle why such ranging interpretation of a text should be unable to move from a scholarly to a meditative mode. No doubt different aspects will come to the fore, but then so they do in different

kinds of scholarly exegesis; and there will be an intelligible continuum of response to the text, resting on the intention of 'listening'. Some will feel that such an element of self-consciousness is wholly inimical to meditative prayer. But the one who prays should surely not give the stamp of inerrancy to his praying thoughts. As he opens himself to God, he is bound to recognize the limitations and distortions which he brings to the scene. In exercising detachment of this kind, he is in line with the sensibility proper in scholarly interpretation. In that sense, prayer of any kind, however fervent and direct, demands an element of self-distrust, an interior brake of self-criticism.

However, the exercise here in mind remains precarious: seeing alternative significances in texts easily degenerates into frank contradictions and the compartmentalizing that we seek to avoid. So we recall continually the serious objective: if we would come before God as made known in Jesus, for in him our commitment is placed, then we have a duty to avoid, to the utmost of our ability, what can be shown to be travesty or inaccuracy in our understanding of him. In moving to the meditative use of the Gospels, we have to maintain a continuum of interpretation in something like the way we have described. The label of prayer is no licence for fantasy.

It is possible to view this continuum in more optimistic terms. We have often had occasion to refer to the restraint which study of the Gospels imposes on both 'natural' and traditional readings of the texts. Such a way of regarding the matter can seem discouragingly negative; as if scholarship (and, apparently, the proper attitude of prayer) should fill us with inhibitions and at every turn stop the free movement of our minds. There is, of course, no denying that enquiry imposes discipline; it scotches our tendency to nonsense and refines our judgment. And the self-awareness that is part of enquiry carries over into our attitude as we pray; as we saw, on such a basis the continuum of interpretation largely rests. Nevertheless, this profitable and necessary restraint is not always of the same character, and its recognition of the limitedness and partiality of all human interpretation is not only a warning but also a liberation. It is a warning chiefly at the scholarly end of the continuum of interpretation: against crude bias and over-confident attachment to conclusions where the evidence is inherently inadequate. But it is a liberation when it comes to the meditative use of texts – not in order to sanction indifference to truth concerning them, but in order to give freedom from scrupulosity where precision simply is not available to us. In this more imaginative activity, recognized as such, there is room for a creative appreciation of the texts, which will not do violence to their meaning, but will enable them to 'speak' more directly and more as 'wholes' than the analytical procedures of some aspects of scholarly enquiry tend to allow.

4. What has just been suggested recognizes legitimate differences of approach to a text; it seeks to accept their validity, and to see a continuum of interpretation along which they lie. We may have to learn, however, not to insist that there is open to us by this means an approach to God by way of the figure of Jesus 'as he was'. The study of the Gospels is far from yielding total scepticism about the Jesus of history, but it remains unclear where exactly accurate information is to be found, and we see that that information is always reflected through the evangelists. Moreover, the boundaries of their contributions to the portrayals which they give are indistinct and disputed. It is unlikely that this assessment will undergo essential change. Obliqueness like this looks like being a deterrent to prayer, a kind of insult to the person who in praying is aware of relation to God by way of Jesus and is not disposed to tolerate anything less. But the interposition of the evangelist is not different in principle from that of ourselves. To recognize the limitedness of our apprehension of the divine and the intrusion we necessarily make, as we move into the picture formed by our act of relating to God, is to recognize the same factors in the Gospels. There could be no such thing as 'direct encounter' with the historical Jesus by means of any conceivable literature that might have been written. Regrets of the kind described here are largely misconceived.

5. Finally, we must ask how far this way of prayer can ever take us. We recognize its complexities and pitfalls. Taking it as an example, we began from the point of its being found attractive, and we have not sought to underestimate its strengths. After all, it seems so essentially Christian to pray by meditating on Jesus. Yet it must always be merely a beginning. In engaging in prayer, we have no business to forget that while God for the Christian is made known through Jesus, he is not made known exclusively by this means. There is, after the journey of imagination to Jesus in the Gospels, the return to the present where God is to be served. In that perspective, we see once more that the integrity of mind and heart which is sought in this book cannot be circumvented.

In discussing the bearing of New Testament study on the meditative use of the Gospels, we have been attending to the area of greatest abrasiveness. Other modes of prayer (notably intercession) are open to questions from a philosophical standpoint and may be refined by careful doctrinal or ethical thought. They are less affected by the specific interests of biblical scholarship, except in its general inculcation of self-criticism and of awareness of the conditioned quality of speech and image-making about God. It is not surprising that people conscious of such limitations are often drawn now towards word- and image-free prayer of a contemplative kind and towards meditative techniques which are designed to foster it.

This awareness gives rise to another difficulty which affects both personal and liturgical prayer. It is at root the moral problem of sincerity. Where prayer is verbal, and particularly in liturgy, it is almost inevitable that it draws upon the Christian past at many levels and stages. Whether the worshipper is aware of it or not, in the course of an act of worship, whose text he may see to be in modern English, he is likely to travel, in a random chronological order, through the whole gamut of periods of Christian history and through a wide range of modes of Christian thought: from a Victorian hymn to a Platonist-cum-biblical creed, by way of a Cranmerian prayer and an early-mediaeval Latin collect, quite apart from scripture readings which may themselves span a millennium. Equally, he may range through language that is literal, metaphorical, hyperbolic and mythological, all juxtaposed and with no signals as movement occurs from one to another. There is then the question of identifying with such a vast and diverse range of material – once innocence is lost and knowledge has entered in. The knowledge may be detailed, concerning the precise provenance and nature of item after item, or it may be general, just the awareness that here is what may well be thought of as cultural chaos, something that grew or was assembled with none of our historical consciousness in mind and with no attempt at homogeneity of thought-form or language.

As just expressed, the situation seems to verge on scrupulosity. Surely the difficulty, as a practical problem, is contrived. In real life, things are different. It is a matter of language having different uses and properly evoking different responses in different contexts. It is possible both to dissect a love-poem in the schoolroom, and then declaim it to the beloved (unless the practice is obsolete), with no sense of incongruity; to learn the lines of a play by sheer slog, then act them, genuinely identifying with the role to which they belong. So it is possible to engage in the historical or conceptual investigation of scripture and of liturgical forms in one setting or mood, then use them as vehicles of prayer and worship in another.

There is, of course, much sense in such a contention, and it rings true to experience. Almost any worshipper who is educated in the materials of worship and does not simply suppress his or her knowledge adopts some such accommodation without undue strain. The original meanings of the texts that make up the liturgy are eclipsed by the significance, only partly verbal, which their use in worship within a whole rite imparts to them. But this leaves a feeling of unease. It is an approach which declines imperceptibly to a point where there is indifference to the content of liturgy, so long as the occasion 'feels right' as a religious-aesthetic whole – at best, presumably, if it serves to focus the worshipper validly on God.

No doubt such difficulties admit of no clean resolution. To see them is at least to begin on the task, and it is an important area where Christian discrimination or the talent of the religious connoisseur, whose formation is perhaps the true objective of a modern education in theology, most appropriately comes into play.

More perplexing still are cases where forms of prayer make confident and terse allusion to ideas which scholarship shows to be blatantly in need of glossing. References to the resurrection or ascension of Christ, to his sitting at God's right hand, or to his future return lie in a territory which cannot satisfactorily be described as dispensable poetic imagery. These matters are not just the language of edifying hyperbole which nobody imagines to have any kind of correspondence with genuine reality. They are, rather, terms which bear upon 'hard' doctrine. Believing worshippers might, on reflection, agree that all of them contain an element of non-literal and mythological statement; but they would also agree that, to varying degrees, they contain important elements of truth, valid pointers to divine reality. They might agree that these creed-like features in the language of worship could be placed on a sliding scale with regard to the degree of both literalism and metaphor or imagery they contain. Thus, Christ's session at God's right hand may be seen as at a different point on that scale than the resurrection. Where there is wide divergence among believing worshippers is over the placing of the scale as a whole in relation to correspondence with reality. So, for some, the resurrection[9] involves a large measure of factuality, even though it also involves interpretation and image-borne ways (chiefly originating in Jewish apocalyptic language) of referring to divine reality; while for others, even the resurrection seems to belong to the area of mythology – a mode of speech about God which has no element of literal truth but uses conventions to express religious conviction. The Second Coming evokes the same variety of response. It may seem to the former group that the others strain sincerity to the limits; and the others may themselves feel that it is artificial and regrettable that the tenacity of tradition in the matter of forms of prayer compels them to pray in words so uncongenial, so needful of sophisticated or oblique explanation if their working is to make any sense at all.

There is one important respect in which the ethos of Christian prayer and modern New Testament study work towards the same end. We saw that this study gives rise to a number of styles of sensibility or priorities of mind which collaborate in those who grasp them. They include: a sense of diversity in Christian life and understanding as no threat to their genuineness and validity; a sense of the artificiality of the division of Christian thought and experience into distinct areas, chiefly those labelled doctrine, ethics and spirituality; a valuing of the 'soft' and poetic rather than the 'hard' and conceptual way of expressing Christian belief; and an awareness of the risks run when Christian thought is divorced from practice, as also when it becomes segregated from general truth and from the life of society. All these convictions about Christian thought and life are likely to spring up in the minds of those who reflect upon the character of Christianity disclosed in the New Testament. We note again that their significance lies not in the fact that the New Testament stems from the origins of the faith, but in the inherent capacity of this study to bring them before us. Once in our minds, they provide stimulus for thought about many areas of present Christian life and experience.

It is not fanciful to suggest that important traditions of Christian spirituality share, in their own mode, many of the aspects of sensibility which we have just described as emerging from study of the New Testament. There, too, we commonly find a reluctance to streamline Christian life into any single expression, a measure of restraint in dogmatizing, and a determination to unify all aspects of thought and practice. Of course there are devastating examples to the contrary; nevertheless, this is not unfair as a characterization of, for example, the more humane traditions in monastic life, especially when they are contrasted with some of the activities of ecclesiastical authorities in the enforcement of orthodoxy. There is enough here to suggest that above all in its single-mindedness, its conviction that the quest for God makes all other concerns subordinate, the tradition of spirituality has often maintained a sense of the priority of our relationship to God which has otherwise been blurred. To put it another way, both New Testament study and the tradition of spirituality can convey a realization that the *issue* of Christian faith is rightly posed at few points and involves a decision on direction which is essentially simple: whether there is a God to receive and serve, as made known in and through Jesus. Such a realization puts most of the doctrinal issues of Christianity into proportion; and it expresses very well the essence of the Christianity witnessed to and striven for in the New Testament.

Religious commitment involves not only prayer and worship. For many, it involves, in one form or another, the commendation of Christian faith in articulate speech. This is certainly another area where modern New Testament study is more often felt to be a stumbling-block than a help. What has the initial promise of being an essential tool for the preacher turns out to be an encumbrance, soon to be laid aside. And yet laying it aside gives a bad conscience. Sometimes there is also protest: to have learnt so much at such cost and to find it so intractable for what seems at first sight its most obvious use is hard to bear.

Some of the relevant considerations are adventitious, quite outside the theological sphere. The decline in any dependable body of Christian knowledge in church congregations, the necessity of brief homilies where there is neither time nor taste for the conveying of information or the building of a case, the partial assimilation of any public speaking now to the mores of entertainment: these constraints are transcended in only a few Christian communities and contexts.

But there are also other considerations to which New Testament study may point the way. It is, for example, apparent that Christian life in the early congregations was more complex and varied than was once thought. The received picture of it has long been dominated by the Acts of the Apostles, a story of Christian expansion, dynamic and irresistible, brought about as a result of fearless and tireless public preaching. And behind that, the standard impression of Jesus' ministry is dominated by the idea of him as one who preached and acted with authority. It is an impression based on Gospel statements,[10] on the fact of the Sermon on the Mount, still often seen as central in the Gospels as a whole, and, at a more academic level, on the perception of Jesus as being in the tradition of the classical prophets of Israel whose manner and activity he revived, and on a picture of early Christianity as essentially kerygmatic in its style of belief and in the presentation of its message.

Yet this is a one-sided picture. There is ample reason to believe that the presentation of the life of the early church in Acts is the servant of a preconceived picture, in which success and public prominence are much to the fore. The letters of Paul and the social realities in which he worked make it probable that his methods were less spectacular than Acts implies and that much of his approach was more a matter of pastoral suggestion and counsel than of proclamation.[11] The gospel picture of Jesus' teaching shows him as working by means of parables, with their evocative and invitatory power, as much as by powerful preaching.

There may be a salutary prompting here to consider whether our models of preaching and of Christian communication in general have not been too homogeneous, too concentrated on the desire to proclaim and exhort, with the authoritative speaker addressing those set to receive his words. Again, it is not that the ways of primitive Christianity are, without further ado, obligatory for us. It is simply that the variety in early Christianity, the suggestion that more than one model of communication was practised even then, may free us from stereotypes and lead us to a reappraisal, in terms appropriate to present need, of Christian communication in our circumstances. There is no reason, for example, why the widespread unease with the quality of preaching and the widespread dissatisfaction of preachers with their lot should not lead to a revision of this whole genre of speech; why it should not be seen as more integral to the act of worship in which it occurs, rather than an oratorical interruption, inappropriately grandiloquent and laden with authority, to the liturgical act; more a coaching in the Christian life and way of thinking than a deliverance of a word from the Lord. No reason why it should be felt to be so strongly obligatory when other modes of communication (such as the liturgy itself) are at least as effective or when other methods are plainly more suitable for certain purposes (such as the conveying of Christian knowledge and understanding). It may be that the sermon itself is better seen now not so much as an exegesis of scripture, for which the time is usually inadequate and the occasion inappropriate, given the technical complexities involved, or as a chance to convey Christian instruction, but rather as an art-form wherein the speaker, in a kind of one-sided conversation with the audience, uses all possible and suitable resources to evoke perception of the Christian way and strengthen attachment to the Christian cause.

Starting from the study of the New Testament and taking its results seriously, we have found some fruitful lines of thought affecting various aspects of Christian commitment.[12] In many ways, they converge with lines that emerged as we saw how New Testament study leads us to think about other aspects of theological thought. It is not impossible to see how synthesis can develop and integrity have a chance to prevail.

In Part Two of this book I shall lay out, in a number of set pieces, examples of issues to which the principles outlined in part one can usefully be applied. The issues are of different kinds, so that the variety of application, which may of course be extended to other matters, can be apparent. They are designed to encourage the reader to do further work on his or her own account.

PART TWO

-7-

Being in a Tradition

This essay considers a subject which comes to the surface time and again in theological and religious discussion: the proper limits of adaptability in Christian belief and life. Everybody now knows that development is continuous and often bewilderingly rapid and unforeseen. Yet everybody hankers after following genuine tradition. The facts of discontinuity and the desire for continuity are unreconciled. In this essay, these matters are discussed, with a touch of exaggeration, in their own right: they have never been far from the surface throughout Part One.

The question is: what does being in a tradition actually amount to? It arose with particular force for me from the experience of giving a lecture on 'The Legacy of Liberal Catholicism', as part of a commemoration of the 150th anniversary of the Oxford Movement in 1983. The lecture treated the subject straightforwardly: an outline of the history and then a few conclusions. The inherent difficulty sprang to mind afterwards. It lay initially in identifying the phenomenon, Liberal Catholicism, which was put before me. Its beginnings were not hard to find: the name belongs first to the group of Anglican theologians responsible for the publication of *Lux Mundi* in 1889. Their acknowledged leader was Charles Gore, who gladly accepted the description of Liberal Catholic. It was an odd description by present-day standards.

In specific conclusions, Gore's liberalism extended to taking the Genesis stories down to Abraham as unhistorical and to treating Jesus' humanity as less wooden and less purely conceptual than it was in traditional christology.[1] It did not extend to thinking that Anglican clergy might preach in Nonconformist church halls or that Anglican bishops need not believe in the virgin birth or the physical resurrection of Jesus – as Hensley Henson discovered in relation to both matters.[2]

But if Liberal Catholicism began in that way at that time, when did it come to an end? Michael Ramsey[3] says it finished at the time of the Second World War – a strange judgment, when many would place *him* firmly in the ranks of the Liberal Catholics – and he is still with us. Michael Ramsey referred to the demise of a certain style of corporate scholarship among Anglican Catholics, and that has certainly faltered and slipped away since the 1930s. One might feel that it had gone awry by the 1960s, when Alec Vidler, surely once a plain Liberal Catholic, edited *Soundings*,[4] which was a good deal more liberal than catholic. Ramsey also had in mind the emergence of what he felt to be the less balanced and more stridently conservative orthodoxies of scholasticism and 'the transcendental theology of the Word in the Bible'.[5]

Ramsey's is only one way of judging the matter. By other criteria, Liberal Catholicism only reached its heyday after the Second World War, above all in the spread of eucharistic worship as the norm in the Church of England. One could also point to the survival of social witness and thought among Anglican Catholics well into post-war years, though it is now certainly weaker than it once was. Both of these were features of the Liberal Catholicism of Gore and his friends. When in my lecture I tried to locate the legacy of Liberal Catholicism now, I had to point outside Anglicanism altogether to figures like Edward Schillebeeckx; though a case was recently put for the continuing viability and desirability of Liberal Catholicism in its original Anglican setting.[6]

What a muddle all that is! Here is a movement of thought, having a number of different characteristics, but relatively short-lived; and how hard it is to identify it with any precision, to be sure whether it has reached an end or still exists, and to know what developments are to count as authentic and what beyond the pale. Perhaps the title of my lecture, 'The Legacy of Liberal Catholicism', was a mistake from the start.

Yet Christians (and others) are accustomed to speak with great confidence of traditions which they see operating over a historical period or which they wish to commend. Some of them are reckoned to have lasted for centuries, even throughout the history of Christianity or beyond it. When I use the term 'tradition' here, I mean of course not particular beliefs or practices but something like a theological approach or ethos with which people identify themselves or are identified, fairly or not, by others. Certainly, when such an approach or ethos is analysed, it can be broken down into or associated with particular beliefs and practices; but it is not identical with them or even with the sum of them. It is not exhausted by a listing of them, any more than Olivia's beauty in *Twelfth Night* was conveyed by a tally of her features.[7] Indeed, the listing may lead the tradition, in this present sense, to disintegrate. As we have already seen in the case of Liberal Catholicism, people may be quite convinced that such a tradition exists and that they or others are part of it, but the persistent common features turn out on enquiry to be few and changeable. On the other hand, *particular* traditions may be shared by groups with no sense of belonging to a common tradition, and may be found on either side of high boundary-fences. There is that about a tradition of the kind I have in mind which raises the suspicion that it is to a large degree a matter of psychological feeling or social convenience rather than objectively identifiable criteria; that is, being in a tradition depends very much on thinking that you are.

For example, in taking the label 'Liberal Catholic', Gore in no way saw himself as breaking essentially with 'the Catholic tradition' as found in the Church of England (with all the mixture of fact and mythology about continuity from earlier times which that entailed). In the phrase 'Liberal Catholicism', that is, the emphasis really fell on 'Catholicism'.

But to his earlier mentor, Liddon, the situation looked quite different. After the publication of *Lux Mundi*, Liddon wrote to Gore in commenting on their respective positions: 'We are not opposed in *this* sense, that I hold all Criticism to be mischievous' (and he points with approval to textual criticism in particular). 'All Criticism, I suppose, really proceeds on certain principles, preliminary assumptions . . . Where do they come from? A Catholic critic would say, "From the general sense of the Church". But a modern "psychological" critic (if that is the right word) would say "From his own notion of the fitness of things, or from the outcome of literature at large".'[8] Liddon there showed himself deeply perceptive. He had realized that, notwithstanding the minimal nature of Gore's concessions to critical, liberal enquiry, a vital line had been crossed, a chasm had opened up, perhaps a tradition had been ended. Gore might think that 'the Catholic tradition' was only modified in accidental features of its being by the moves which he had made, merely adapted to aspects of new knowledge; but there was as much to be said for Liddon's view that the developments signalled such a break that the discontinuities far outweighed the continuities. We may leave open the question whether Liddon had overestimated or Gore underestimated the seriousness of the change, and simply note that whether you are in a tradition or not depends very much on whether you feel that you are. It can be as subjective as that. Or to be more precise, it depends what elements in a tradition are regarded as essential, as actually constituting it, and what elements are expendable. Liberal Catholicism has been our example, but we know full well that the Benedictine tradition, the tradition of the Archbishopric of Canterbury, and the whole Christian tradition itself would have served just as well and raised the same questions.

We may wonder how it is that people can set as much store as they plainly do by being in a tradition, when the whole idea is so indefinite and riddled with holes whenever it is inspected. Is Robert Runcie in the tradition established by Augustine in AD 597? Clearly yes, if you count mere succession in office and episcopal activity in Kent. Plainly no, if you count papal authorization as of the essence. Very much no, if you think of beliefs, outlook and social role: a room containing those two prelates together with, say, Dunstan, Becket, Cranmer, Laud and even Howley or Tait, would soon be a babel of mutual incomprehension. It is naive to wonder at people's attachment to being in a tradition, because people are greatly open to self-deception when it comes to establishing their identity and importance. We all need to place ourselves in the universe, and recognizing an inherited past is an important way of doing it.

That explanation would almost suffice if awareness of being in a tradition were merely a matter of comforting private fantasies and official rhetoric. But in Christian theology, it has played a much more significant part than that, as it often has in more general historical perception. From at least the beginning of the second century, and arguably from Paul onwards,[9] Christian writers were strongly aware of themselves as in an articulate tradition, above all a tradition of teaching, and saw themselves as the latest heirs of a process whose story they could trace. Irenaeus may be seen as the first classical exponent of this awareness,[10] but he is neither the first nor the last to hold it.[11] His particular importance is to show us at any rate one reason for its prominence. In essence (though the instance was more momentous), it is, in relation to our present interest, the same situation as that which we have witnessed in the case of Liddon and Gore. To appeal to one's position in a tradition is one way of vindicating one's teaching against that of others who think differently. Irenaeus did it by appealing to apostolicity: the inheritance in continuity of the apostles' doctrine, office and mission. It was of course *his* version of that appeal as opposed to that of others, in particular the leading Gnostics. *He* saw the thread of teaching from the first days coming straight through to *his* hand, *they* saw it coming through to *theirs*. And who are we to say that either side was anything but sincere in its conviction? It is true that the Gnostics appealed to *secret* tradition, which may be a sign of insecurity about their doctrine, but it may equally be a sign that only secret tradition had for them the cachet of authenticity. To us, it seems that both were developing and modifying whatever they inherited from the early days, and most of us would say that the Gnostics had travelled much further than Irenaeus. But then, we are heirs of Irenaeus' victory; and who is to say that the perspective which makes it seem so has greater validity than that which made a Gnostic teacher put forward his claim to apostolic authority?[12] More sharply (because the case is more extreme), is it self-evident that the writer of the Pastoral Epistles is more faithful to the Pauline tradition than Marcion – and by what criteria could a decision be made?[13]

Or, to take another, even earlier case, long masked by the cover of canonicity: Luke's Gospel preface (1.1–4) shows both deference to his predecessors, whoever exactly they were, and a frank determination to improve upon them. He is aware of being in a tradition, and, while less afraid of being innovative than Irenaeus, is in no way wanting to go against those who wrote, albeit imperfectly, before him. But to us, he seems to have produced a portrayal of Jesus very different from Mark's, if one follows up its theological and religious implications.[14] And how can we now, in the light of our redaction-critical sensibilities, estimate what it means for either Matthew or Luke to be handing on a tradition established by Mark (assuming they used him), except in the formal sense that they wrote books of roughly the same shape and subject-matter? It is only with hindsight and under pressure of controversy that the perception of oneself as in a tradition becomes important, and undoubtedly, in the case of the evangelists who were following predecessors, the present was the yardstick by which the past was measured. The past (both the life of Jesus and any earlier evangelists) was the lackey of the present (the later evangelists' situation) rather more than the present was the handmaid of an authoritative past. And so, in Christian history, it has largely been, as Robert Wilken so stimulatingly showed.[15]

The situation seems to be this. To make ourselves out to be in a tradition all but necessarily involves us in falsifying the past. Why then can we not be content to be ourselves in our own time, just accepting the various connections of thought and company which convince us and appeal to us? Ah, but we *are* in continuity with the past in innumerable ways, and we do exist in a whole network of traditions, ranging from styles of cooking to ways of praying to God; and our present habits are a tangled web of old and new, too tangled to be satisfactorily unravelled. We are in a bewildering condition.

Undoubtedly, Christians at all levels on the whole find any such admission not merely of important innovation but of confusion profoundly disturbing. True, they have reformed their liturgies because it was felt that as they stood they were out of touch with popular habits of speech and behaviour; but the new liturgies were a great deal more marketable – and perhaps only marketable – because it could be claimed that they followed the earliest models and went back to Hippolytus.[16] Of course the claim was in many respects inflated, as Hippolytus would recognize if he found himself at a modern eucharist. It referred largely to the liturgy's shape; but there is much more to forms of worship then their shape. Again, we work for reunion between our various communions, but say we are bidden to do it by alleged New Testament injunctions, just as those who made the divisions in the first place also appealed to other New Testament biddings. Whatever we do, it seems, we must show we are in a, even 'the', tradition, deceiving ourselves at every turn, by our partiality even if not our barefaced falsification.

At this point, it is worth noting that concern to be in a tradition can express itself apart from any explicit awareness of the successive stages of a continuous process at the end of which is oneself; rather, it is often a matter of being knit up with the beginning – the fount of the tradition alone counts. This may carry with it (or derive from) a belief that in the time between things have declined from the pristine model; but it may exist quite apart from that belief. Awareness of the tradition is simply confined to those two moments: the beginning and the present. The First Letter of John is the first Christian instance of it, with its transformed use of 'beginning', to refer to the start of the Christian movement and not, as in the Gospel of John, to the beginning of all things or even some eternal 'moment' or state which is anterior to and above all that is.[17]

In cases of this kind, the tradition has a clear-cut and apparently uncomplicated attraction. It is easy to see the past, originating moment as recaptured, re-actualized in the present, as for example when the eucharist is perceived as a reliving of the Last Supper or a vivid recalling of Christ's death, or both together. Clearly, in such a case, nobody can claim identity, and nobody quite sets up the eucharist as a passion play: what is happening is that *elements from* both the past event and the present rite are abstracted and made the bearers of the tradition. It is the basis of that abstraction which merits examination, for it carries all the weight on which existence in the tradition is constructed; and, once more, it often reveals the present much more than the past, and the past dances to the present's tune.

The compelling recognition that we deceive ourselves, for the sake of comfort and of providing ourselves with authority, is modern, and even those who recognize it cannot always live by their recognition. Earlier generations, whose historical awareness made discontinuities a difficulty for their determination to be in a tradition, solved the problem in their own ways. Peter Brown notes how Newman, thoroughly conscious of the constant flux of historical change but setting up as the apostle of the teleological thrust of theological development, was able to relegate much of what fitted badly into the main stream of the tradition to the level of the popular: 'The religion of the multitude is ever vulgar and abnormal; it will ever be tinctured with fanaticism and superstition, while men are what they are. A people's religion is ever a corrupt religion.'[18] Brown is concerned to point out that such division of a social and intellectual context is misleading. In particular, he shows how the cult of the saints in late antiquity, so embarrassing to many later Christians at least in some of its aspects, was integral to the perception and sensibility of a whole society, from the top downwards, not the dispensable nonsense of credulous rustics. In other words, it cannot be maintained that discontinuity exists at the bottom of the Christian heap, while the bishops or theologians keep the pure tradition going.

Yet is is also true that we *are* in a tradition, or rather in a whole muddled network of traditions. Perhaps I can, with time and patience, sort out what I owe to, or share with, this or that figure or movement of the past. But I must recognize two things: first, that my synthesis is new. However faithful I may reckon to be, and wish to be, to the Liberal Catholic tradition, the Benedictine tradition or any other tradition, I am pressed constantly to amend and develop it, and I may seem to contradict and do it down; I can only do it with a better or worse grace, a greater or lesser wisdom and self-awareness. And second, that it is *my* perception of that past which is involved. I have no reason to suppose that those whom I follow, in whose tradition I reckon to be, would support my estimate of the situation. What I see as faithfulness, they might easily see almost as treachery (as Liddon did over Gore).

But granted all that, do I have a responsibility to the traditions in which I stand? And if so, what is its character? I have used in passing the example of the Benedictine tradition. A witness worth interrogating on this subject is David Knowles, whose life was dedicated to the understanding and proper perpetuation of that tradition and to a struggle against fellow-monks who, in his view, were false to it.[19] At what level should such a dispute be conducted? Is there any profit in carrying it on at the lofty level of the attempt to define 'the essence of Benedictinism'? Or is it more candid to work at the pragmatic level, that is, to ask, in the light of all present circumstances, what life here at *this* monastery should now be like? Plainly, part of that discussion involves an appreciation of the contribution of the past, for the sake of sheer identifiability. As a matter of common sense, if a Benedictine monk I am to be, then there are continuities to be observed, or my aspiration is meaningless; but the continuities are not to be drawn from some mythical perception of the heart of Benedictinism or a view of the Benedictine life at some allegedly ideal stage in the past.

Then there is the bigger question. Is what I suggest for Benedictinism or Liberal Catholicism (supposing anyone is concerned to preserve it) viable for Christianity as a whole? One could mount a case for saying that, behind all the talk and ink-spilling about continuities, the more pragmatic style of behaviour I have described is the one we adopt in fact and in practice. What people really care for is not so much faithfulness to the past as their own security in the present, and they draw selectively from the past what will, without undue inconvenience, minister to that need. We are compelled to solve the problems confronting us in the present, however great our sense of continuity with the past (whose problems were different), and whatever the parallels which might edify or admonish.

These things are true theologically as much as at the level of practical decision-making. In that sense, the attempt to be in the tradition stemming from Jesus, or from the primitive church, or from Chalcedon is futile if it means seeking to perpetuate without significant change what they are alleged to have stood for (though admittedly one man's significant change is another man's trifling alteration). Is it not more candid to say that one feels a prime responsibility towards the present, with its questions and issues; that the past is there to be drawn upon and that one finds stimulus where one may and as one finds most truly appropriate; and that being a Christian involves finding that stimulus in the Christian past? This is, of

course, undeniably, one way of 'being in a tradition', but it is a
frank and relaxed way: that is, it accepts membership of a
community as the fundamental mark of identification and
involves no feeling of compulsion to insist on this or that
element of continuity as essential to identity – chiefly because
such insistence is impossible to substantiate and proves
illusory.

Chiefly, but not solely because of that. There is also a more
theological justification for such a proposal. I scarcely know
how to put it without sawing off the branch on which I have
chosen to sit.

However you view it, Christianity began with some combination of continuity and discontinuity. We cannot be clear
how much to put in each category and what weight to give to
each. Suppose Jesus himself is the object of attention; suppose
he was, roughly but precisely enough for our purpose, an apocalyptic prophet. Then his being a prophet was drawn from the
past – he was entering into a tradition. But his message was for
the present, in view of an overwhelmingly dominant future.
That is, the past served as no more than a provider of a land-
mark, a religious and social identity. What mattered about
Jesus was not what he inherited but what he initiated. Soon,
however, the balance changed. Even Paul, than whom few if
any early Christians had a stronger sense of the imminent End,
was nevertheless tortured by the desire to be, despite the
evidence to the contrary, historically and theologically in the
tradition of Israel.[20] Perhaps, in fact, the same was true of Jesus
– we cannot say. The question of how to be in that tradition
worried early Christianity to the uttermost and it is possible to
analyse the New Testament writings as a series of responses to
it. Each of them is different: for people can never agree how to
express their participation in a tradition, even when they are all
convinced of the importance of belonging to it.

Let us suggest that that issue, on any showing one which
most of us can now either ignore or view more dispassionately,
never deserved the vital significance it then received. The

distinctive mark of Christianity, that which gave it the impetus to be a new faith, was, as Paul (partly) and Marcion (purely) both perceived, its concern with present and future. From that point of view, the constant turning to the past, whether Jewish or ecclesiastical, for authorities rather than for landmarks, is a profoundly distorting change of front. The concern with present and future might be characterized as resulting from a simplicity of trust in God, a sense of his immediacy, and a readiness to accept the here and now as his and as the scene on which he must be met and served. But now I begin to preach the virtues of a somewhat austere tradition in which one may be content to stand.[21]

-8-

What to Believe about Jesus

Christology has not lacked attention in the last ten years. There is much uncertainty about the perspective in which to view it. Above all, in this area the historical and the conceptual relate uneasily. In this essay, there is an attempt to consider the subject in the light of the principles outlined in Part One. So it is a 'worked example', whose approach could be used elsewhere.

The term christology is regularly used in two different senses. Which sense is intended depends on whether the context is that of New Testament studies or that of doctrine. Here, I start from the former but look outwards to the latter, intent on working towards some kind of synthesis.

When the doctrine specialist talks about christology he is usually trying to state the terms on which Christ may be understood as both human and divine. If Christ is not held to be at all divine, then the question of christology does not arise; and if he is not held to be at all human, then, though there could be (indeed, has been) christology of a sort, it would now be so unusual as not to merit serious consideration; this would, of course, rule out incarnation, which is normally the heart of christology as doctrine sees it. In this doctrinal context, christology often seems to be the attempt to solve a problem, which is generally put in twofold form: How can the one God be understood as differentiated, so that as the Father is divine, so is the Son, not to speak of the Spirit? And, how can the eternal divine Son exist humanly, or, alternatively, how can Jesus of Nazareth be one with the divine Son? Putting it in terms of a problem along these lines does of course presuppose at least a measure of canonizing of the late patristic discussion – that which preceded and surrounded the achievement of the Council of Chalcedon in AD 451. And the historian might say to the student of doctrine that to set the task in this way is to be the slave of one stage of one particular line of development. He might say that there is an adventitious quality about that line of development. In those cultural circumstances, in the atmosphere of later Platonism, it turned out so, but the task might be seen in other terms, and doctrine ties its hands too tightly if it is seen as the solution of a problem posed in this way.

Indeed, the doctrine specialist himself might, perhaps with a degree of apostasy, be glad to get out of this rigorously problem-solving idiom and to admit that it is indeed a legacy of a period of Christian reflection which was peculiarly philosophical in tone. Feeling that, he might re-state his task in other terms, which are looser and more obviously religious. He might say that his aim is to elucidate the deep Christian impulse to yield worship to Jesus: an impulse felt to involve neither impropriety nor taint of polytheism; and that he seeks to give an account of Jesus, seen as central for our relationship with God, in the light of and in connection with his understanding of God himself. In other words, christology follows from theology (in a strict sense of the term) and springs from Christian experience. He may even wish to leave ambiguous the word 'our' in the phrase 'central for *our* relationship with God': does it mean everybody or just Christian believers? That is, does it allow for a pluralism of faiths or envisage, whether stridently or gently, a Christian monopoly?

For the present purpose, I wish to see the task of christology in these more relaxed terms. It certainly does involve a task – less rigid and demanding than in the more philosophical, classical approach, but still an identifiable task of conceptualizing, with an eye open towards religious experience and even the practicalities of religious life. But it has to be acknowledged that in this less rigorous style of christologizing, the idea of incarnation in a strict sense is liable to be a casualty.

When the New Testament specialist talks of christology, he means something quite different from the exponent of classical doctrine, and it will help to define the doctrinal task more clearly still if it is seen in relation to the conventions of New Testament study. According to those conventions, what goes by the name of christology may include *any* belief about Jesus and centres on (though it is not exclusively concerned with) the elucidation of the titles accorded to him by the New Testament writers (son of God, son of man, lord, messiah, word, etc.). Now of course with hindsight, that is, in the light of the later development, these titles may be seen as adumbrations of what was to come, and it is in terms of some such purposive, evolutionary perspective that a blurring of vision often occurs; but it is clear that none of these expressions arose in pursuit of a christological task in the sense that classical doctrine understands it. They arose out of an experience and conviction of Jesus' centrality for relationship with God and show scarcely a sign of a clear or formal *problem* needing a solution (either in relation to monotheistic faith or to the connection of divine and human in Jesus). Apart from the Fourth Evangelist in his reflection of controversy with Jews and the writer of I John insisting against fellow Christians on Jesus' humanness, hardly any New Testament writer shows much sign of explicit doctrinal quandary in that sense.[1] In other words, even the highest claims made for Jesus were seen as responses to him, the man, though of course to him, the man, who, as no other had done, mediated God's purpose and presence. There is no question of an incarnation of God in the strict, problem-raising sense.

I think the point is simple and uncontroversial: that the New Testament writers were, however audaciously in some cases, working out from experience of Jesus, whether earthly or, now, exalted, and not from a theoretical need to elucidate a problem about God and the bearing of Jesus upon divinity. In this light, we might say that the New Testament is more in line with the relaxed version of the doctrinal task which I outlined.

But that version has weaknesses which the more rigorous and traditional approach to christology warns us against: it almost dissolves christology as an identifiable task altogether. Christology easily, in a modern historical perspective, turns into a mere statement of the obvious: that Jesus is central for the Christian understanding of relationship with God. That is a statement not of doctrine but of observable fact. To make it 'doctrine', perhaps it needs only the addition of: 'and God meant it so'; but that is still exiguous by way of conceptualization. And though the terms or indeed the range of questions may now be different and more uncertain, those who are attached to the classical doctrinal manner have a right to say that Christians must explain their attachment to Jesus much more coherently and fully.

Yet in recent years, christological writing has been shying away from any such explanation. Consider the period since the publication of *The Myth of God Incarnate* in 1977.[2] Given the outcry it occasioned, you would have thought that the world was full of clear-sighted Chalcedonians ready to produce a reasoned defence of traditional orthodoxy (that is, christological doctrine in the classical mould). There has been plenty of *assertion* of the traditional doctrine, but reasoned argument has been in short supply. Quite the contrary; there has been what it may be wicked to call a quiet victory of the main contentions of *The Myth* by osmosis. Writers claiming attachment to traditional faith have come to express themselves in terms essentially at one with the main thrust of mythographers'[3] teaching. Even in *Incarnation and Myth*,[4] which resulted from a conference held a year after *The Myth* and consisted of the original mythographers and an equal number of theologians of other views, it is not always easy to tell who belongs to which side: that is, if traditional classical christology is your yardstick.

It is particularly striking in the short book of essays, edited by Anthony Harvey, *God Incarnate, Story and Belief*.[5] The title promises a treatment of strong orthodoxy, but not a single essay gives a reasoned theological account of classical christology. Some assert reasoned traditional faith, it is true: but the central essays, by Harvey himself and by Vermes, give an account of what may be affirmed about Jesus as a historical character. Not differing widely on that, the one sees it as, both then and now, the sufficient ground for Christian commitment, the other as leading to no such inference. Only perhaps in C. E. Gunton's *Yesterday and Today*[6] has English scholarship produced an extended treatment of traditional christology written as a work of doctrinal argument.

It is not hard to see why there is such a dearth of cogent and reasoned christological statement. As a recent writer[7] put it, 'historical method is intrinsically hostile to claims of metaphysical uniqueness'; and, with both those approaching him from the side of the New Testament and those whose interest is chiefly doctrinal, the historical approach to Jesus seems to have become dominant. Sometimes it emerges as the only conceivable approach, sometimes as a blockage across the path of christological thought which there is no clear means of either circumventing or turning to advantage. On the basis of the historical data about Jesus, viewed as the fruit of historical enquiry and judgment, how can christological faith be other than just that – an act of faith? As an act of faith, it may indeed be both legitimate and understandable. It does not fly in the face of the evidence, as it would, for example, if historical study showed Jesus to have been a fraud or quite nondescript. But neither is it compelled by the evidence in any demonstrable fashion. In that sense, faith is arbitrary. One man will have it, another not, and it will be the result of factors other than simply the plain demand of the evidence.

Writers quite diverse in the elaborateness of their treatment[8] give us in effect a critical account of the story of Jesus and the early responses to it, expressed in first-century terms, and invite our judgment. Here, surely, doctrine, in any traditional sense, has been eliminated. What we have is on the one hand history and on the other hand faith, as man's response to the history. It is no wonder that christology, as a subject of enquiry or, as in the terms used earlier, an area of problem-solving, may appear to have vanished.

There has been a shift of sensibility here in recent years which is not always grasped – and, of course, not shared by everyone. A response to the points I have just been making might go as follows. The New Testament itself does not give us simply historical data about Jesus or even, more accurately, material which, properly understood, helps us towards histor-ical data about Jesus. It gives us the fruit of reasoned reflection on Jesus in the light of belief about God. It may not be, with the possible exception of Johannine christology, anything that you could call philosophical or logically coherent. It works, in effect, more by way of powerful images which are juxtaposed, having been re-minted as a result of their application to Jesus. 'Son of God', 'son of man', 'messiah', etc. all 'work' in this way. But nonetheless they constitute christology – and we can appropriate them, we can set about believing as they believed and articulate our beliefs as they articulated it. This was, of course, the basic contention of the biblical theology which flourished in the 1940s and 1950s and was so influential in the liturgical revival of that period and since and in the work of Vatican II.

But for many, its appeal has faded. Schillebeeckx,[9] for example, emphasizes that good theology always works with two poles: Christian origins on the one hand, but on the other the Christian present, that is, the cultural setting in which faith must now be articulated. The trouble with biblical theology was then that it mistook an act of imagination for an act of appropriation. We can see, enter into, the faith of the first Christians, but, once we understand its terms, itself requiring an imaginative act, we are likely to recognize their alienness – their distance from us. And, however much they nourish us, we cannot feel dispensed from the task of speaking of our faith in terms closer to home and of more general currency. Then, in what terms? If the culture we live in does not readily reflect upon the likes of Jesus and is at ease, when it comes to thought about him, only in asking historical (and perhaps psychological) questions, it is no wonder that christology (i.e. doctrine about him), as distinct from faith in him, vanishes. What is there to talk about? What language is available?

If this were the end of the matter, there is no doubt that there would be some theological benefits, especially in the area of inter-faith relations, notably in relation to Jews and perhaps Moslems. Jews, who often share Christians' culture as well as some parts of their religious inheritance, commonly state their objections to Christianity's special claims in terms which identify it with the classical trinitarian and christological pattern. That *is* Christianity, and that they cannot believe. But adherence to Jesus, even belief about Jesus expressed in less metaphysically ambitious terms, is more widely comprehensible, less outrageous to others who share monotheistic faith.

So christology is in danger of being a vanishing subject, or at best perhaps a fossilized subject: it may go on being believed and discussed, but in terms which isolate it from other, even related, areas of enquiry. Some of its language will undoubtedly persist in the sphere of liturgy and preaching, as expressing, as it were in slogans, warm faith in Jesus; but that is not the same as extended, rational statement. In that sphere, its role is greatly diminished and (it is empirically observable) fast disappearing.

Most of the recent authors referred to have contributed to the process but without acknowledging it. Indeed they have tended to affirm the contrary. In that sense, the demise of christology is like the quiet slipping away of an old person while his companions chatter away and even talk optimistically about their friend's continuing life. But some have dared to point frankly to the truth. Both Maurice Wiles and Dennis Nineham, in their contributions to *The Myth*, raised the question whether, with the passing of the traditional metaphysical scheme, Christian doctrine would not in future have a unified, single focus, i.e. God himself, rather than the dual, or threefold,[10] focus of traditional treatment. We may note that C. K. Barrett, doyen New Testament scholar, can hope for a 'better understanding . . . that the NT . . . is in the end about God'.[11] Clearly, many factors point in this direction and some of them have already been mentioned, above all the continuing preoccupation and fascination with the history surrounding Jesus, which both by its very existence and by the uncertainty of its results makes the raising of metaphysical edifices seem a perilous business. Equally powerful has been the wide perception that the classical pattern was, in its heart, mythological, in the sense that it tells a story bringing things divine and human, heavenly and earthly, into the framework of a single, homogeneous, essentially seamless account; and, as mythological, inadmissible as an objective account of reality.[12] In particular, this realization meant the removal from the sphere of literal, biographical truth, to be spoken of in the same continuum as Jesus' birth and death, of the assertion of his pre-existence – which was the very lynch-pin of the classical scheme. Abandon that, and the trinitarian problem does not arise; and trinitarian doctrine, if it is to survive, must be transported into a new, non-mythological key; the christological problem too, seen as the uniting of the eternal Logos with human nature, disappears, for the eternal Logos is mythological, in almost every sense of that over-used word.[13]

Moreover, historical awareness not only affects knowledge about Jesus but also our understanding of the nature of the first christological claims. We see that Jesus was *christos* or *son of God*, for example, not in the sense of occupying an office, like Lord Mayor of London – an office waiting to be filled, whether in God's arrangements or merely those of Judaism; nor in the sense of receiving an honour, like a medal or a peerage, or, to give a closer analogy, a royal dukedom conferred from birth on a member of the House of Windsor; but in the sense that, in the culture of the time, this was an appropriate expression of acclaim or commitment. It derived from human faith, not celestial officialdom.[14] And if a title carried with it, from its existing Jewish use, the idea of heavenly existence, as *word* (*logos*) did, then of course pre-existence[15] came to attach to Jesus, as part of its sense; but its nature was the same – it was an expression of human acclaim. Only subsequently did its use as myth (i.e. as part of a full-blown story) or as metaphysics (i.e. as part of a speculative scheme) – and the two categories are barely distinguishable in this context – come to the fore.[16] While such an understanding of origins does not of itself invalidate the development, even in the use of the same terms, it certainly creates unease and a sense of relativism where formerly there were claims of unchanging being.

For all these and other reasons, christology dissolves – either into historical investigation or into the bare, even if fervent, affirmation of faith. And not everyone finds it easy to maintain both those substitutes. No wonder one or the other is liable to be neglected or abandoned, for they make an incongruous pair: the one demanding a cool, impartial spirit of enquiry, the other a warm commitment of life.[17] The summons 'Who is on the Lord's side?' accords ill with an insistence on stopping to examine the precise nature and merits of the cause.

The situation is far from satisfactory. Not only does it leave, formally, a wide gap between historical talk on the one hand and religious talk on the other, creating a sense of their incongruity: but also, intellectually, there is a space demanding to be filled. That space can only be labelled 'doctrine'. As we have seen, we live in a time of uncertainty about how to fill it. Try and do it with the traditional pattern stemming from patristic times, and the sense of incongruity is only heightened: now we have not two but three discrete and diverse elements in our talk about Jesus – and that cannot be an improvement. But try and do it in any other way in a culture so unsure how to speak theologically, and there is a tendency for the alleged doctrinal material to move towards either the historical or the religious, there to be assimilated. Much christological discussion centring on New Testament categories falls into the former category, landing up as part of the attempt to characterize the historical Jesus and the claims made by and for him; much christological discussion centring on symbolic or abstract statements concerning Jesus merges into devotional language about him and, while natural as the speech of religious response, is unhelpful in the attempt to understand; it is imprecise, and baffling when it comes to making links with the historical data. So there is a space demanding to be filled: to be a Christian is to accord to Jesus unique significance in our relationship with God; so that, if faith is to be rational, christology needs somehow to survive. But it is not easy to see what material to use in order to fill it.

Students of the New Testament may make a contribution if they will dispose their minds suitably – that is, if they enquire not simply what the New Testament writers meant by the words they used (in this case concerning Jesus) but what was 'going on' as they used them. Such students are after all, quite well placed. It is their business to study the historical data. To that side of the matter they have devoted, some say, too much attention and too rigorous a scepticism. But the character of the New Testament material is such that, if they choose, they may also view Christian origins in a religious light. The New Testament literature is a literature of religious response; and in it, the historical, the religious and indeed the doctrinal are inextricably fused. Our present task is, then, one to which they are accustomed – at any rate, in the setting of Christian beginnings.

So what was 'going on' as the New Testament writers began to express their experience of Jesus in words? It has been customary in the past[18] to approach New Testament christology by way of the titles accorded to him, taking them as independent terms which then found themselves included in the Gospels or letters of the early writers. The emphasis then tends to fall on various aspects of New Testament christology, viewed as a whole. There is, of course, a certain validity in this method, but it may be helpful to adopt a different one. Focus instead on the New Testament writers in turn. Each brings his own mind to bear on the theological enterprise. Each is limited and determined, for the character and terms of his response to Jesus, by the education he has received and by the workings of his unique mind. His christology is, in the end, *his* christology – not simply the result of random fishing in a common pool.

To clarify the process, I invoke the idea of what may be called 'mediatorial space', the intellectual and emotional totality which lies between a person and God as he looks towards him. There can be little doubt that for all the writers (except perhaps that of the Letter of James), the effect of Jesus had been total and comprehensive. It had left no corner of their worlds unaffected. True, not everything had been abandoned or even transformed, but where elements of their previous outlook had remained virtually intact (aspects of Jewish practice, lists of virtues and vices, catalogues of household duties), they had at least been set in a quite new light. And in all central matters, concerning their view of the world and of history, of themselves in relation to God and each other, and above all of God himself, the effect of Jesus has been decisive. But that effect was different in each case, in style, range and content. It differed according to the style, range and content of the convert's mind before his conversion or perhaps as his Christian discipleship proceeded. We may express this by saying that for all of them, Jesus was the mediator, filling all the available mediatorial space, but that for each of them the extent and character of that space was different according to his existing perception of God and his relationship with him.

For example, for a Jew whose sense of relationship with God was wholly and exclusively formed by the Law, and to whom Jesus had become the transforming and saving agent – *the* mediator – it would be both inevitable and wholly satisfactory to see Jesus only as the giver of a new Law. If this Jew's horizons really were limited in this way, he would be incapable of seeing him in any other terms and have no incentive for doing so. In seeing Jesus thus, he would be receiving what was for him salvation, entering *his* new world.

Or if our Jewish convert had instead been fervent in his messianic hopes, if his religious horizon had been exclusively filled with expectation of a new age inaugurated by a messianic figure, and if (by whatever means) his life had been seized by Jesus in the chemistry of conversion, then Jesus would inevitably be seen as the messianic inaugurator of the new world which the convert knew he already, in some sense, inhabited. Jesus would be seen in those terms and no other terms.

Now the range of possible examples from the world of Christian origins is very wide. None of those represented in the New Testament is as simple as the two theoretical cases we have examined. They are in fact complex: the religious horizon in each case has a number of distinct, though interlocking, features. But the principle is valid: each has his picture of mediatorial space, to him total and comprehensive; to us looking from outside, partial and limited: and for each, Jesus, the transforming mediator, has occupied that space.

We may of course be inclined to grade them, and accord to some higher marks for comprehensiveness, for extent of mediatorial space, than to others. Thus, for the writer of the Fourth Gospel, on the basis of an existing 'wisdom' theology or the like, the range of Jesus' significance is as wide and as old as the universe itself and his role and being as profound as those of God; and it *must be so*, or else Jesus would not be occupying all the mediatorial space in the writer's conception of things. That is, the writer would be expressing a response to Jesus which was less than total. He would be saying in effect: 'Jesus has done *this* and he has done *that*, but he has not done everything', or, 'He has affected *this* part and *that* part of my world, but not all parts.' And to leave out the cosmos would of course be quite an omission! Not that the Fourth Evangelist leaves the matter there: Jesus steps not only into the role of the creator-word, but also into the role of the Jewish law, the word's voice, as well as the Temple and the feasts of Judaism.[19] That tells us the range and nature of the writer's mental 'world'. Jesus fills it all, occupies all the available mediatorial space.

To this writer, we are inclined to award high marks; higher than, for example, to Matthew who lacks the cosmic dimension and to whom the notion of Jesus' pre-existence did not occur – his mediatorial space was different in character and extent, so the idea did not arise. But this procedure seems to be lacking in historical realism and sympathy, and to lack propriety. It arises, of course, out of hindsight: it just happens to be the case that certain aspects of the Johannine view were fertile for later patristic development.[20] But as a whole, it belonged in its own day very much to one part of the Jewish world. So there should be no question of higher or lower marks. Matthew, John and the others all work on the same principle, each letting Jesus fill his horizon; and each has his own validity and right to exist.

Some of what has been said may seem to imply that Jesus' role in the scheme outlined is much too passive, as if it were being suggested that he was conformed to the existing needs and thought-patterns of the believer. It does not take a cynic to say that much in the history of Christian devotion to Jesus (not to say christology) can easily be taken in that way. But by no means is that a fair account of the matter, with regard to either the New Testament or subsequent developments. There is a process of transformation of which Jesus – what he was and signified – is the agent.[21] That is, in terms of the present discussion, the mediatorial space of the convert or disciple is itself re-shaped as Jesus enters it. An early Jewish convert, whose mind centred on the Law, does indeed come to perceive Jesus as the giver of a new law, but it is Jesus, the crucified and risen one, who acted and taught thus and thus, who is that law-giver. His law-giving is marked by his whole character and career, and he gives new meaning to the very ideas of law and law-giving, though it may still be true that such a convert has little in his religious equipment with which to deal theologically and constructively with aspects of Jesus outside the range of his existing perception. While in this way all christology, from the very beginning, has its inevitable element of subjectivity and therefore distortion, there are responses to Jesus which have a much greater immediacy than others – that is, where it is plainly Jesus and not some figment of religious imagination who has occasioned transformation of the believer's mediatorial space.

Our principle does not apply only to the New Testament, but equally to each succeeding christology, in the patristic period and since – in so far as that christology seeks to articulate a genuine conviction concerning Jesus as the saving agent who has, for the one concerned, transformed his world and so filled the space of which he is aware. If Jesus has not had this effect for him, then his christology is likely to be seen in terms of formulas authorized by others, rather than in terms that are 'real' to him.

This principle may also give us the clue to seeing what christological statement is valid for us. If it is to avoid the error and fantasy which have bedevilled so much thought in this area, it must start from such knowledge as we can achieve of Jesus himself – not always precise and detailed knowledge, because not much of it is to be had, but knowledge of the general thrusts of his message and his style of life, knowledge that he stood for *this* rather than *that*.[22] There is every reason for us to pursue the quest for this knowledge as rigorously as we can, using all available tools of historical study. It will also stem from the religious conviction that through Jesus our 'world' is different, in all sorts of complex ways but in all its aspects, from what it would otherwise have been (or, if we are converts from other beliefs, from what it was before); that through Jesus our relationship with God has the character which it has come to bear.

The question of doctrine then poses itself thus: how may this religious conviction find expression, in relation to my total understanding, on the basis of what I know of Jesus? What is the range and content of my 'world' which either has, perhaps inarticulately, been transformed as a result of my commitment to him, or needs to be so transformed? What exactly is my mediatorial space which he can fill? Like the New Testament writers, each will make his own response to these questions, each have his own areas of concern which form his 'world'. Again, as in the case of the New Testament writers, these areas will overlap, so that there is consensus as well as distinctness; but in our very diversified culture we should be unwise to try and insist on too much consensus. For some, the area of effective or central concern is that of personal relationships; for others, matters of political or social policy and behaviour. To each, Jesus will bring his presence, by way of the colouring, critique and transformation of what preceded him.

The christological procedure here outlined invites three reactions. The first is that it is too subjective, too fragmented, too uncontrollable to merit consideration as doctrine. As far as the diversity[23] is concerned, there is truly no way of avoiding it in our present cultural situation: still relatively new in terms of the Christian theological tradition, it is something we have to learn to make sense of and not just bewail. And the subjectivity, too, seems inevitable: we cannot now avoid asking what is 'going on' as we conceptualize, and what goes on happens in our human heads. Uncontrollable, too: the element of consensus is some consolation to those who feel vertiginous in the face of the lack of clear criteria in modern doctrinal thinking. For the rest, a Christian thinker must simply cultivate discrimination and humility.

The second reaction is that, to use terms adopted at the start, the classical doctrinal problem has not been solved – or, putting it another way, incarnation has disappeared. But, on the view I have taken, the 'problem' posed in christology, classically seen, is in fact a creation of one perception of the mediatorial space filled by Jesus: and that perception, belonging to patristic times and their long legacy, brought incarnation, in the strict sense, along with it. It is a wonder, properly intelligible only within the patristic pattern where it found its articulation. Outside that pattern, if it is held, then it must be, I think, as a sheer wonder, a *magnum mysterium*, attracting faith and love but defying reason: in my terms, religion but not doctrine. Incarnation is, then, one way of seeing the place of Jesus, not *the* way. Yet the role of Jesus, as the bridge-figure, remains intact.

It is tempting to speak of such a pattern as that presented here as involving an attempt at the restatement of classical orthodoxy, but that is misleading. It is not as if we are to treat that orthodoxy as a norm which all other forms of teaching must somehow set out to reproduce. It is itself one member of a series. And it is not clear quite what 'restatement' is in this context: classical orthodox christology needs classical orthodox words and can stand no others.

The third reaction is that this essay has not given 'doctrine', 'teaching' at all, but only a little elementary hermeneutical enlightenment. There is no need to cavil much at that; in an unmetaphysical and pluriform atmosphere, 'doctrine' is a strange, uncertain kind of exercise. Moreover, explanation of and reflection on what we do as we articulate our religious convictions is an important kind of 'teaching', even if it may not merit the use of its somewhat tougher synonym 'doctrine'. Chiefly, the aim has been to bring into smoother connection historical investigation about Jesus and the business of having faith in him, and to have uttered a kind of doctrine which is not far removed from either.[24]

-9-

The Resurrection

There are many excellent books about the resurrection of Jesus.[1] Most of them are written from either the historical or the doctrinal side. In no way does this essay need to duplicate that work. So, in the spirit of Part One of this book, the subject is presented as another kind of worked example, following that on christology. There is a summary account of the main factors and arguments that must come into a discussion of the subject, then some conclusions. As in all of this book, these follow only if the considerations previously raised are digested.

The importance of the subject is undoubted. Here more than anywhere else in the programme of Christian beliefs, history and doctrine, texts and ideas intertwine. Frequently it is claimed that Christian faith is impossible without belief in Jesus' resurrection; less frequently are we told exactly what is to be believed. But it seems impossible to dispense with either 'event' or 'idea'. Many have felt that in this respect, the resurrection and the incarnation are in parallel. The latter cannot do without belief in the virginal conception of Jesus, any more than the former can do without the empty tomb.[2] But there are probably more who see their way to belief in incarnation and feel that the story of the virginal conception is just one way of speaking of it, problematic, inessential and even misleading in some respects, than there are who can give any meaning to the resurrection unless the gospel stories are, at least broadly, true.[3] This is therefore a point of crucial intertwining of history and doctrine. In what follows we shall have to consider not just the issue of the resurrection in itself, but the whole matter of taking it as a belief in its own right in the customary manner.

Direction: There is no better subject than the resurrection of Jesus to illustrate the point that data once seen as straightforward testimony to events now come before us as evidence whose nature and worth we have to sift.[4] This key shift in sensibility affects not only our perception of the historical evidence itself but also our understanding of the contexts of meaning in which people have seen the resurrection. We shall first give a brief account of the historical aspect, then turn to the main doctrinal ideas associated with the resurrection. As factors come to be discussed, an attempt will be made to assess their value and status.

The historical evidence: Broadly, the evidence is of two kinds. There are statements of the resurrection as a fact, as in I Cor. 15.12ff. ('Christ has been raised from the dead' will serve as a paradigm), and there are stories associated with it. The latter are all in the Gospels, at least one in each of them, but there are statements in Paul where a story is implied, as in I Cor. 15.5–8. None of this evidence is first-hand. The nearest is Paul's claim that the risen Christ appeared to him within, but at the end of, the series of appearances which he recounts (I Cor. 15.8; Gal. 1.16); but there is at least a possibility of special pleading here. He may be stretching a point (as he is stretching the period of time involved) to have his own crucial experience counted in with the earlier experiences, and it is open to doubt whether his 'appearance' was generally admitted to be of the same sort as its predecessors. As for the stories, it is clear that they stand some way down a process of tradition. While Paul, confining himself virtually to bare statement, testifies to very early belief, especially in his inherited credal formula in I Cor. 15.3ff., the stories in the

Gospels all come, in their present form at least, from the last thirty years of the first century.

Both stories and statements testify to appearances, but differ about their nature: are they 'physical' or 'spiritual'? The distinction is not wholly clear. The argument of Paul in I Cor. 15 (cf. v.44; and Gal. 1.16) implies that he believed the latter; though the term 'spiritual *body*' creates a doubt. Some of the Gospel stories state the former. Luke, for example, is explicit: 'a spirit has not flesh and bones as you see that I have' (24.39); though his physical Jesus is able simply to appear in closed rooms and then to vanish. All the same, at least one of Paul's implied stories, the reference to an appearance to five hundred brothers, may be taken, not unfairly, to suggest objectivity. Oddly, it leaves no clear trace in the Gospels.

Taken together, the stories and the statements bear witness to two kinds of happening, linked but distinguishable. There are appearances, to a number of individuals and groups in a variety of places, and there are testimonies to the empty tomb. The earliest evidence, in Paul, relates exclusively to the former (I Cor. 15.4–8), though 'that he was buried' (v.4) may well be taken to imply knowledge of, if not exactly attention to, the emptiness of the tomb.

The earliest story we take to be that in Mark 16.1–8. It tells of the empty tomb but contains no appearance, the very reverse of Paul. Yet, like Paul, it has a hint of that which it does not describe: an appearance is promised in Galilee (v.7). All the later Gospels have both elements, appearances and the empty tomb, and in a number of stories the two combine, so that the distinction we make between them may be simply a feature of modern analysis and not necessarily bear upon the origin or development of underlying tradition. There is legitimate scholarly disagreement here. Partly because Paul is earlier than any of the stories and is explicit only on appearances as testimony to the resurrection, it is often suggested that the tradition of appearances has more credit than that of the empty tomb. However, given his Jewishness, it is highly unlikely that for Paul there could be belief in resurrection which did not involve Christ's body, and the argument of I Cor. 15, taken as a whole, implies it (though the *risen* body is 'spiritual).

Statements are not common outside the writings of Paul, though I Peter is an exception (cf. 1.3, 21). In Hebrews, for example, the resurrection (as distinct from Christ's exaltation to heaven) is mentioned only in 13.20, and is rather deliberately bypassed in 12.2. It is possible that some early Christian circles dwelt more on Christ's present heavenly status than on stories about his manner of arriving at it, and the widespread use of Ps. 110.1 as a proof-text may have encouraged such a perception. It may be that Paul looms larger in our canon of scripture than he did in the Christian life of his time.

The *stories* in the Gospels may be classified in two ways. First, there are features which occur in different forms (some related, some perhaps not) in different Gospels: e.g. delayed recognition of Jesus (Luke 24.16, 31; John 20.14; 21.4); women (or a woman) at the tomb (all four Gospels; Mark 16.1–8; Matt. 28.1–10; Luke 24.1–11; John 20.1–18); young man/angel/ angels at the tomb (all four Gospels: Mark 16.5; Matt. 28.2; Luke 24.4; John 20.12); the physical reality of the risen Jesus (Luke 24.39, 42f.; John 20.20, 25, 27); appearances in Galilee (Mark 16.7; Matt. 28.10; John 21.1ff.; but visibly suppressed or diverted in Luke, cf. 24.6 in relation to its Marcan parallel and model); appearances in Jerusalem (Luke 24.13–53; Acts 1.3; John 20.11–29).

Second, the resurrection stories in a particular Gospel may be viewed, not as having emerged from the tradition of such stories circulating as a distinct genre within the early church, but as part and parcel of that Gospel's whole narrative pattern and theological outlook. Thus, Mark's brief story (16.1–8) looks back to many earlier passages, e.g. 8.31; 9.31; 10.34; perhaps 9.1; 9.9; 14.51f.; 14.62; 15.40, 47. In general, its enigmatic quality is characteristic of the writer and must be assessed and understood in the wider context. Or again, Luke's fine long story of the Emmaus walk is full of Lucan motifs: a journey, a meal of fellowship, the fulfilment of scripture, the wonder of the aura of Jesus' presence. In John 20, we have the motif of the relationship between Peter and the beloved disciple, as in 13.23f. and 21 (contrast Luke 24.12), and reminiscences of John 11, where once more interpretation will test for connections of thought. Matthew seems to have no independent tradition to report, apart from the Jewish tale that the disciples stole Jesus' body, which he worked into and around the story he inherited from Mark. His final verses (16–20) are formal, and they are less a resurrection story than a strongly Matthaean tableau which includes most features of his essential doctrine (Jesus and the church as teaching, Jesus as sovereign and as authorizing disciples to carry out the mission, Jesus as present with his own until the End).

The historical evidence is, then, complex, diverse, indirect, and essentially obscure. No amount of faith or church authority can, as we now see, alter its character or increase its force. We can analyse the narratives in the Gospels, pointing to theological features and literary connections, and the more they strike us, the less assurance we are likely to have that they represent history directly. We can note the historical statements of Paul about appearances, though we cannot tell exactly what he believes about their nature. None of the evidence takes us close enough to the origins for a historian to say with assurance what happened, though he may well hold that something must have happened along these lines: very soon, faith took the raising of Jesus as the great divide.

It is often alleged that the very fact of the church's survival of the crucifixion of Jesus itself testifies to the truth of the resurrection, though hardly to any specific account of it. The point is often put in the strong form that the church's very existence rests on the fact of the resurrection and can be explained in no other way. It is a weighty argument, but even this historically based claim is far from being beyond question.

There are instances of religious movements transcending such devastating defeats by way of the experience of new-born hope, not without similarities to that given by the resurrection of Jesus.[5]

The historian can go no further, except that even within this part of our enquiry it is pardonable to note the disjunction between the obscurity of 'the resurrection' (so that we cannot even say precisely what it was alleged to be) and the massive claims made about its significance. It is also pardonable to wonder about the nature of a God who would make as much as is commonly claimed depend on a happening as difficult as this even to identify, let alone interpret. Could belief concerning such a happening really be an article on which Christian faith and our salvation hang?

Interpretation: It is not the 'happening' which constitutes doctrine, but the 'happening interpreted'. Clearly, even if events at the root of the resurrection faith were as plain as could be, it might be understood in ways that did not in the least amount to theological doctrine: e.g. it could be taken as a para-normal experience, or as an inexplicable quirk in nature; or else in theological ways which did not amount to *Christian* doctrine: e.g. as a demonstration of divine power worked upon Jesus, a prophet of God, comparable to miracles occurring in the career of Elijah, or to the Koran's view of Jesus' virginal conception and ascension. The alleged miracle of the resurrection of Jesus does not of itself carry Christian meaning with it, but needs 'placing' in the context of other and Christian beliefs, especially about God's way of fulfilling his purposes and about the identity of Jesus in relation to that work.

Our concern is with Christian interpretations given to the happening. It is important to note that the plural must be used: There is no single meaning that Christians have given to the resurrection, and we cannot, with precision, speak of '*the* doctrine of the resurrection'. It is also important to see that it is better to think in terms of *contexts of interpretation* rather than simply *interpretations*. Ideas concerning resurrection do not stand isolated from settings but spring from wider or deeper beliefs and relate to them. The significances given to the happening are intelligible only against their various backgrounds.

In the light of these considerations, I now list some of the chief interpretations which have been given to 'the resurrection', from the earliest ideas open to our examination.

1. Whatever happened in the sequel to the death of Jesus, it is clear that it lent itself to early interpretation in terms of *resurrection* (though, as we have seen, not exclusively so). It is equally clear that such an interpretation means that it was placed within the context of Jewish apocalyptic thought, where, in certain strands, resurrection was an important element.[6] At the End, there would be the resurrection of the dead, together with the judgment, the vindication and eternal blessedness of God's righteous ones and the punishment of the wicked. In various ways, a number of early Christians not only looked to such an End, with Jesus as its agent, but also saw in his ministry on earth, and above all its momentous climax, an anticipation of that state of affairs within the world's present course. Thus, Paul saw Christians as already in part transferred to the coming age, to which, in customary thinking, the End of this age would lead. Already, one might say, 'resurrection' had embraced them, or had at least begun to do so; though its fullness still lay ahead,[7] as his argument in I Cor. 15 shows. But that argument, and indeed this whole framework of ideas, is established on Jesus' resurrection: the first-fruits, the guarantee of the resurrection of his followers. What they would receive fully at the End, he had already received in being raised by God on the third day after his death.

As far as it goes, the pattern is striking and consistent. It does not, however, answer all questions: as we have seen, it is not wholly clear how 'physical' a resurrection he thinks Jesus had experienced. On the one hand, resurrection of the body is, as in Jewish writers, the basic idea with which he chiefly works; on the other hand, I Cor. 15 suggests that for him the raised or 'spiritual' body is as different as it could be, short of loss of identity, from the mortal body of this life.

Paul's working so tightly within the apocalyptic sphere of discourse, in which resurrection ideas find their origin and are at home, also raises the question how much sense can properly be made of resurrection outside that sphere. It may seem that, far from being an independent concept, relating to Jesus (and then to those who believe in him), it is tied to that cluster of concepts and that programme of events by means of which God is seen as bringing his purposes to their fulfilment. In that case, the problem is: once we are aware of its place in that nexus of ideas, what can it mean when taken apart from the rest, and what can we mean by 'believing in' it unless we hold to the total apocalyptic 'package?' This is a fundamental difficulty with making sense of the resurrection. Within its original context of ideas, we can see that it fits wholly and convincingly. Outside it, it becomes – what? Perhaps a mere wonder, a free-floating miracle, drawing the attention of those who believe it by its sheer stupendous quality, but lacking a meaning. And because powerful beliefs cannot long rest in that state, then it is on the look-out for other meanings. Such other meanings have not been wanting. But is such an idea/happening as this entitled to go a-hunting in this way and to find new modes of intelligibility?

2. The writer of the Fourth Gospel already found himself (not consciously, surely, but in the logic of his work) in some difficulty on this account. His procedure was to maximize the concentration in Jesus, as presented in his ministry, of the characteristics of the new age which would, in Jewish belief, follow the End. In other words, he carried further the process already apparent in Paul. Thus, Jesus in his life-time *is* the resurrection (11.25). Also, glory and exaltation, both themes associated with the future age and with heavenly life, are used in explication of Jesus' death by crucifixion, in powerful paradox.[8] At Christ's death, all that must be done has been done (19.30).

The price paid by the writer for this doctrine is that themes naturally associated with the resurrection have been used by the time he reaches it in his narrative. So while the resurrection is in no way underplayed as an event, the meanings given to it are somewhat secondary – when compared with its necessity in Paul to the whole effectiveness of God's saving plan, whereby Christ's death-cum-resurrection bring the new age to bear within the declining fortunes of this present world. For the Fourth Gospel, the emphasis falls instead on the physical reality of the risen Jesus, the giving of the Spirit, the place of faith which lacks 'sight' of Jesus, and the roles of Mary, Peter and the beloved disciple.[9] It is worth noting that the resurrection is never referred to at all in the Johannine Epistles; the emphasis on Jesus' humanness, the major thrust of John 20–21, is put in ways that need no reference to it. Clearly, it was not at the surface of the mind of the member of the Johannine church who wrote those letters a few years after the composition of the Gospel.

So, for the writer of the Fourth Gospel, 'resurrection' as an event is verbally assimilated to Jesus' death, and as a doctrine it is an important way of speaking of the believers' union with Jesus, depicted normatively in his relationship with disciples in his lifetime but persisting. In that way, 'resurrection' is union with Jesus now, 'eternal life' as given (5.24; 11.25).[10]

3. We have already seen that the stories told of the risen Jesus contain a number of distinct motifs. These are often interpretative in character or theologically significant. For example: in Luke, as in John, the physicality of Jesus is probably brought out to counter docetic tendencies, which Paul's 'spiritual body' doctrine may even have served to encourage; eucharistic fellowship with Jesus is seen as still available in the church (Luke 24.13ff.; John 21.1ff.); Jesus reigns from heaven over the world (Matt. 28.16–20); and it may be that the position of women in the early church helps to dictate the prominence given to them in the resurrection stories.

4. In the patristic period, the apocalyptic pattern was no longer the prevailing idiom of thought, and the resurrection received other interpretations. For Athanasius,[11] Jesus rose to demonstrate his victory over death: his resurrection was 'a monument of victory against death', and he delayed his rising until the third day in order to refute the charge that he had not really died. The theme of victory over death made an appearance in Paul (Col. 2.15), as an image subsidiary to the overall apocalyptic context. But now it acquired a more independent and central role. Above all, it brought Jesus (and then his followers) immortality and physical incorruption. Indeed, participation in them was already possible in this life, through reception of the sacrament of Christ's risen body.[12] The two great ills of the human lot as then perceived, mortality and corruption, were thus overcome. It was also a victory over idolatry, of which Athanasius saw the living proof in the triumph of Christianity, just recently as he wrote, over paganism.[13] These were the ways the resurrection then felt on many Christian pulses.

It may, however, be asked what the logic is in such an interpretation. What does 'victory over death' mean when death is still all around? Is that a valid or realistic way of describing the church's position of strength in the world, as in the time of Constantine, and the longing of believers for life on the other side of deaths which would be real enough? Or is such language a hyperbolic expression of hope and faith? And what is the precise force of *bodily* resurrection in relation to such a supposed victory? What does it 'say' that belief in life after death does not? Apart from the publicity value, so to say, what does the resurrection of Jesus state that his sharing in life beyond the grave does not? Finally, what is the effect when cultures arise in which the horror of physical corruption is not much felt and death itself has lost a good deal of its sting?[14]

5. In recent times, there can be little doubt that 'the doctrine of the resurrection' has effectively shifted its ground once more for many people. Remnants of apocalyptic patterns, which

from early times had moved away from their original role, have now virtually disappeared from lively belief and piety, or have become assimilated into belief about life after death. Easter is now the feats of (*a*) a general hopefulness, and (*b*) assurance of future life in the renewed company of loved ones. The former is doubtless a form of one of the most profound and creative products of the whole pervasive force of Judaeo-Christianity. Its *dependence* on the resurrection of Jesus is harder to demonstrate, once the apocalyptic pattern is lost. It is notable that one of the most helpful and powerful treatments of the theme written in recent years pays scant attention to Jesus' actual resurrection from the tomb as a basis for this way of faith.[15]

As for the latter, it is far from the concerns of the original proclamation of the resurrection. It is, popularly, a matter of immortality of the soul rather than resurrection of the whole person; a matter of a property, even a right, of the self rather than a gift and act of God, and of reunion with loved ones rather than being with Christ. Its tendency is, in effect, to carry the New Testament stories of Jesus' resurrection appearances towards the realm of spiritualism: they *prove* that there is a beyond. Resurrection from the tomb has no necessary bearing on such a context of meaning. It becomes at best a symbol of convictions that can stand without it.

Of course, it is possible to resist these tendencies; but what is to be said instead? The apocalyptic 'package' can scarcely be given new currency. Then is the conclusion for those convinced of the 'happenedness' of Easter Day, that God acted in line with an apocalyptic pattern of thought, which was necessary in that setting for the intelligibility of his act, but is now seen as limited in that respect? Is the conclusion, further, that what was then done no longer carries intrinsic force but is at most a compelling icon of the ultimate power and creativity of God? Yet many a mere theist would have little quarrel with that. So, taken in itself, the resurrection comes to seem no more than confirmation of what, for religious believers of many kinds, is not seriously in doubt. Such belief may well, of course, be shaken by deep adversity, of which the death of Jesus was an example as far as his followers were concerned. But, in such a context, once again the resurrection becomes a local deed, done to serve the needs of the moment. Its purpose was then immediate, as was its true intelligibility. What ensued was the endlessly fertile life of an icon, appealing to the imagination of many in situations, both of thought and of circumstance, which gave to it new meanings and new power to speak of the creativity of God as known through Jesus and of the validity of trust in him, whatever the appearances. And so it is, until this day.

The history relating to the resurrection is obscure, its interpretation is manifold. Often it is hard to understand the sense of the meanings given to it and held as doctrine. Once more, it is not easy to see that something so problematic can bear the weight which is so often placed upon it. Could God make so much rest on this? Should Christian believers do the same?

Or should the whole matter be otherwise conceived? There is much to be said for seeing Christian allegiance as response, not to one or another aspect, but to the whole impact of Jesus. The New Testament writers vary so much in where they place the centre of that impact – in his teaching, or his death, or his coming, or his person, or his resurrection, or in some combination of them – that we may feel that Christian faith is best stated, if we are to give a general account of it, in terms of reception of God as made known through Jesus in his whole presence and career.[16] 'The resurrection' may then take its place as an icon of the fact, inescapably involved in faith, that this Jesus is the focus of hope and life. But it is the *whole* career of Jesus, including his teaching and death, which determines the character of that hope and vitality. This way of regarding the matter at least has the merit of ruling out the common tendency[17] to see Jesus' resurrection as somehow cancelling out his death and ensuring that the story has a happy ending. It rules out, too, that kind of attention to 'the risen Christ', as an object of independent devotion, which is the breeding-ground of all manner of triumphalism, the nourisher of qualities the very reverse of those that mark the life of Jesus.[18] Willing openness to the impact of Jesus-as-a-whole should frustrate such results.

This essay itself suffers, in another way, from the same weakness, for it too has treated the resurrection as an isolated subject. But clearly that is a false perspective, and the matter cannot be left there. Though the resurrection raises its own questions, concerning both history and belief, its role has been, in broad terms, the relatively homogeneous one of illuminating and encouraging Christians in maintaining hope in the face of all kinds of hostile forces, supremely in the face of death.[19] If, then, we come to think that 'the resurrection' should not be the bearer of such a weighty role, can the role itself be sustained? Can hope be justified?

We have seen that treating the resurrection in the traditional way has often led to spurious hope – triumphalist or euphoric hope that simply ignores the appalling realities of so much of the human lot. It is the hope of springtime that wishes simply to forget the winter. Knowing those realities with part of itself, Christianity has often behaved as if they could ultimately be brushed aside or compensated for. The career of Jesus-as-a-whole forbids such easy slipping into the mood of spring. The conviction that 'all shall be well' can never, on the basis of Jesus, be cheaply bought. On the basis of Jesus, it is an ultimate hope held to in the very teeth of suffering and diminution. In relation to death itself, it must be a hope that resists spiritual, intellectual or psychological *dependence* on the assurance of bliss to come: trust is to be in God alone, for his own sake, not for possible benefits. To give allegiance to him with benefits chiefly in view is to vitiate the allegiance. 'Though he slay me, yet will I trust in him' (Job 13.15) has to retain all its force for Christian consciousness, if it is not to sink into frivolity in face of the realities of the world as God permits it to be.[20] Whatever is believed about 'the resurrection' must not be such as to mitigate that force and cheapen that awareness.

We saw that in its origins the resurrection faith was part and parcel of a conviction that the last days, as foreseen in apocalyptic, were in process of realization and soon to be consummated. In its totality that conviction was not borne out by events. How then can we, looking back to its fervent expressions in the New Testament, respond to it? We cannot appropriate it literally and directly without absurd naivety and indifference to all we know of cultural change and the development of ideas. Simply to ignore it, as if it had never been, while appropriating only more congenial elements in the New Testament writings, is to make the New Testament merely serve our present convenience rather than 'listen to' it in itself. Rather, we recognize in that conviction of the first Christians an act of audacious and total hope in the very midst of life's unintelligible ambiguities of pain and joy.[21] To be given the chance to make that hope our own, even unto death, is one of the most significant legacies of earliest Christianity to its successors, with their multiplicity of idioms and circumstances. It is a hope that has often not been grasped, partly because literal adherence to the terms of the first days has obscured the spirit within. Modern New Testament study, by way of painful realism about history and about beliefs, leads us to do better.

Before we end, however, it should be noted that there is another way of looking at the resurrection to put alongside these lines of argument, which have been generated from a starting-point in New Testament study. Suppose we start elsewhere – in the idea that the providence of God might will to *demonstrate* to the eye of faith the guarantee of his presence and of the fulfilment of future hope. Then, within this world, such a demonstration cannot occur apart from some cultural context: happenings do not occur in no setting at all, though they may find ways of being received and evaluated beyond them. What more appropriate happening could there have been than one describable as the raising of Jesus from the dead, and what more suitable initial context than Jewish apocalyptic? It gave a setting for the birth of the new life, but did not detain it for ever. The patristic writers were then not amiss, when, in detaching the resurrection largely from its original apocalyptic framework, they saw it, in effect, as a *demonstration* of the victory of God in Christ.

This way of arguing for the resurrection as essential to Christian faith has been pursued with vigour in recent English theology by Austin Farrer.[22] There is a need to test this approach to the matter alongside the more historical approaches to which New Testament study is more apt to direct the attention. The believer must make choices, and must first decide whether much or little is at stake. It is on that point that revolution first threatens to arise.

-10-

Ethical Decisions and the New Testament

Two of the chapters in Part One were devoted to the movement outwards from the study of the New Testament into other areas of theological thought and practice. This essay is similar, in that it considers some of the implications of modern New Testament study for Christian decision-making in ethics. It is placed here, among the more self-contained pieces of Part Two, because it stands on its own as an argument. It has the useful function of recapitulating, in relation to its subject, the whole argument of Part One. As an exercise within this book, it serves its own purpose, while corroborating the rest. No one will deny either the importance or the difficulty of the topic.[1]

When Christians, whether as individuals or groups, face ethical questions, there is an instinctive tendency to turn to the Bible. There is, however, no great clarity in understanding how help can be found there. It must play a part, it is in some way an authority; but what part should it play?

The complexity of the history of Christian appeal to the scriptures in this area is daunting, particularly with regard to the Old Testament, where there has been great variety and confusion of method. Here, appeal to a text in Mosaic law as directly applicable to Christians;[2] there, its use in an allegorical or analogical sense,[3] quite removed from the original meaning;

there again, appeal to the general tenor of the moral strictures of the classical prophets,[4] or to a theory of fulfilment covering the relation of the Old Testament as a whole to the Christian dispensation.[5] All those methods are already discernible, at least in embryo, in the writings of the New Testament,[6] as they tried to define their relation to Israel. But there has not been, then or since, a clear, agreed answer to the question of the force, for Christians, of the ethical provisions of the Old Testament. No single method has been consistently applied. Nowadays, that most commonly followed is the appeal to 'general thrusts', especially in the moral teaching of the prophets, found so congenial by Christian preachers and reformers. Applicability to modern social conditions is easier to see here than in the regulations for an alien cult and society found in the Law. Nevertheless, it is not unusual to find direct appeal to particular texts, even from the Law, on some specific question where the modern interpreter finds them attractive, though the method is rarely applied consistently and its use fails to convince.[7]

Many Christians, who recognize that appeal to the Old Testament has serious difficulties and so steer clear of it, especially on detailed matters, feel that it is a quite different matter with the New. Those who hold a strong doctrine of its authority will appeal readily to any part of the text, and even those who do not are found making direct and unambiguous use of the teaching of Jesus in the Gospels, as if no question of interpretation arose.[8]

All this is simply descriptive of current practice, found in cases as diverse as the reflection of individuals faced with moral decisions, preachers or pastors giving guidance to those in their care, and official committees helping to form the mind of the church on some issue of current importance. The question remains: on what principles should use be made of the New Testament, in the light of what is now to be understood as truth concerning it?

At the outset, we should recall that we live on this side of a revolution in perception in relation to the New Testament.

Whether we accept or reject its results, the revolution has occurred, and those results are present to us all. Its character is familiar, but it is worth sketching its outline once more, especially in its relation to ethics.

Over by far the greater part of Christian history, the use of the New Testament in this area has been prescriptive. Scripture commanded and it was for the church to obey. As we have already seen, this was far from meaning that its use, though simple in principle, was straightforward in practice. How could it be otherwise? The ethical material in the Bible is not set out in the form of a code, and, even without a historical view of the text, divergences between one part and another are evident. There had to be interpretation, from the earliest stages of the church's history. And even before methods of interpretation, whether of the Old Testament or the New, were formalized, changes of circumstance forced changes in the handling of moral problems. We can see such change already within the New Testament itself. From the very start, with varying degrees of compulsion, there has had to be casuistry: the application of existing provisions to new cases – and often their virtual abrogation in the process. Only on the most general matters (be loving, be humble, be merciful) can such adaptation be avoided without running the risk of intolerable rigour or inappropriateness. In general, the prescriptive use of the New Testament has been subject to a process of adaptive tradition. Church wisdom has interpreted and selected.

We may illustrate from the early period. On the question of divorce,[9] as found in the teaching of Jesus, Matthew, for reasons not known to us but presumably related to the circumstances of his congregation, amended the provision found in the Gospel of Mark: there was to be no total exclusion of divorce, for it could be granted to Christian husbands on the grounds of fornication.

More far-reaching was the almost immediate move towards ambiguity and contradiction on the subject of the possession of wealth by Christians.[10] A major theme in a number of early Christian circles was antagonism to riches and the embracing of poverty. Already in the oldest Gospel, Jesus is shown teaching the abandonment of property as a condition for becoming his follower.[11] Missionaries of the kingdom, going out on behalf of Jesus, are to live with the utmost simplicity. With modifications, this position is echoed in the Gospels of Matthew and especially Luke, where it is a major interest, as it is too in the Letter of James.

Yet it is equally clear that almost from the start of the Christian mission, at any rate from the establishing of urban congregations, this position could not be maintained. Whatever may have been practicable in the Galilean ministry of Jesus and in the itinerant work of his immediate followers, town churches were dependent on their richer members, and on the continuing, stable affluence of those members, for houses to meet in, for resources for common meals, and for the support of needy members. Such a situation is present already in the work of Paul,[12] whose moral teaching refrains from anything more stringent on this matter than the urging of generosity. Generosity is very different from self-beggary; indeed, to be generous a person must retain resources. In the work of Luke, presenting the teaching of Jesus in the circumstances of the late first century, there is probably a duality of perspective on the subject of wealth, which is so prominent among his concerns. In extolling the poor,[13] he may well have had his eye on the rich among his readers, for whom the gospel is indeed bad news unless they let themselves be stirred into shedding at least a substantial part of their wealth and into almsgiving as their constant duty.

By the time of Clement of Alexandria, late in the second century, such adaptation found its theoretician. In his treatise on the story of the rich man who came to Jesus, the distinction is drawn between the possession of wealth and the possessor's interior disposition towards it.[14] What is required of the Christian is not its wholesale abandonment, but generous almsgiving and achieving an attitude of detachment. It is a much more comforting doctrine, dictated by the church's practical needs.

Finally, with regard to family life. The teaching of Jesus,

again prompted by the need for decision in the light of the imminent kingdom of God, makes plain the duty to renounce family ties.[15] Such renunciation is a prime condition for discipleship. No doubt it reflects the situation in the earliest period and, in some circumstances, for many years to come.[16] Yet it was not long before family life came to be reckoned as itself a sphere for Christian virtue, an accepted part of stable church life.[17] Thereby, one ethic displaced another, one total attitude of the self to the world and its responsibilities gave way to another. Of course, in various ways, both attitudes have constantly co-existed in the church. Nevertheless, that early movement from the one to the other was a crucial adaptation, a profound shift in ethical sensibility, under pressure of circumstance.

All the same, the prescriptive role of the New Testament and of Jesus' teaching was formally intact, until the advent of historical criticism. But as the historical approach to the New Testament has become more and more acute in its perception, so the prescriptive principle has increasingly been called in queston. Though it is far from extinct,[18] in terms of theory it has been rendered obsolete; for, as we saw in another context,[19] no amount of scriptural authority can banish the facts concerning the historical particularities of the New Testament writings.

The effect of historical study is to set the ethical material of the New Testament in a fresh light. The settings in which it arose come before us, as do the influences which went to form it. We see it not as addressing us in a tone of command but as recording the solutions which early Christian groups reached to the problems facing them, and we understand those solutions in relation to those specific problems: we do not universalize them. The effect is to distance the New Testament material from ourselves, and, if we do turn to consider it in relation to us, to bring out the discontinuities at least as strongly as any continuities we may see. A brake is placed on the easy taking up of even seemingly timeless and general imperatives like that to love: its 'flavour' and its context in the New Testament cannot thoughtlessly be taken to be identical to those of today. Even within the New Testament and within one church represented in its pages, we witness a shift in the meaning of love between the Gospel of John and the First Epistle, a later product of the same community.[20] At the former stage in its life, the ideal of the Johannine church in obedience to Jesus was the mutual love of its members, seen as reflecting that between the Father and the Son: 'a new commandment I give to you, that you love one another' (13.34). It was a noble and high ideal, even if, we might say, too inward looking – for love for outsiders receives no mention in this Gospel. But when division overtook this church, love narrowed as horizons foreclosed. With all his fervour and sometimes sublimity of language, when it comes to loving, the author of I John draws the line when it comes to those who disagree with him on the content of faith.[21] 'Love' has changed its meaning by the emergence of a new sphere of hate. Even in such a small sphere as the Johannine church, virtue is neither general nor absolute nor timeless, but related to circumstance.

What reactions have there been to this revolution? What attitudes are available, when it comes to the use of the New Testament in making ethical decisions?

We have seen that the prescriptive approach is still vigorous. Untenability is rarely a mortal disease in theology and often the patient never notices it. Some follow the old way wholeheartedly. Others make modifications, in effect taking on board some implications of historical study; but with their attachment to doctrines of scriptural authority, they are hindered from achieving clarity of method or consistency of outcome.[22] Still others, who do not believe in the prescriptive approach, slip into it, especially when strong views on a subject prompt them to it or the rhetoric of pulpit or of controversy carries them into it. In certain settings, it takes a great deal of courage to stand up to even outrageous applications of impressive texts. Taken strictly, this method leads to hopeless inadequacy, as supposedly relevant passages are simply implausible in relation to present circumstances and as moral problems arise for which no biblical text is available.[23] It is not surprising that this approach fares better in the sphere of private than of public morality, where changed conditions are more apparent. The difference in this respect is in fact delusory. The oldness of the past and the newness of the present are universal facts, whose truth must be allowed for in every case, even if in the upshot the continuity with the church's first days comes home with striking power.

The opposite policy, the abandonment of the New Testament as a moral guide, is also common. It is adopted with varying degrees of deliberation. It may be held, for example, that because of the revolution in approach to the Bible, the ethical material in these writings has no force for us, above all when it comes to specific or detailed problems. Life then, including Christian life, was so different that their solutions cannot help, much less dictate, ours. Moreover, the eschatological context of belief, in which the ethical ideas of early Christians were shaped and by which they were pervaded,[24] is not shared by us; so that, however impressive or moving we find their moral thinking, it can only affect ours obliquely and, in many cases, has no bearing on our different framework of belief.

But often, the ignoring of the New Testament is reached by much less considered means. It just feels outdated, it is hard to see ways of making it apply, and our ethical attitudes are adequately and strongly shaped by other forces – the conventions of our social group, the media, the fashions of the day. Christians are no less exposed than others to the pressures of the times, and it is significant how the absence of tools for relating in some intelligible way to the New Testament leads ineluctably to the absorption, despite intention and even protestation, of the prevailing ethos. So the moral positions of Christians of different backgrounds are more like those of their contemporaries of a similar social milieu than those of their fellow-Christians.[25]

An attitude which avoids both extremes, and so seems attractively sensible, is that which appeals to the *general thrusts* of New Testament ethics as still straightforwardly authoritative for the present.[26] The particularities of its handling of detailed issues are admittedly dated, but its broad principles retain their strength. So, the authority of the New Testament is safeguarded and an element of prescriptiveness is entrenched, as are the undeniable fruits of historical study. It is a policy more attractive at first blush than on closer inspection. Who is to decide what is a general thrust and what a detailed issue? Where the modern ethos and the biblical teaching are in conflict, which has the edge in determining whether a general thrust is at stake? This guide is too fragile and uncertain to sustain the role assigned to it. Moreover, the approach lends itself to taking refuge from difficulty in 'thrusts' which are more and more general, as if fleeing from gunfire by darting from one cover to another. The effect is to increase generality to the point of platitude or vacuity. To discover that the Bible urges goodness is to deprive it of usefulness, for we knew that truth already, and of its distinctiveness as a practical moral guide. As when supplied with moral absolutes, one is left with all the detailed work of analysis and application still to do.

Worse still, such a policy does not meet the real force of historical study. 'Thrusts' are as much conditioned by time and place as detailed judgments. Along these lines, there is no escape from the revolution brought by historical enquiry, with its detachment from doctrine.

However, there is something residually and persistently attractive about the appeal to continuing general thrusts whose power is not to be deflected. The flat denial of the principle immediately shows it: it is hard to imagine a Christian ethic which set no special value on mercy, humility and self-denial, qualities which would be high on any list of 'thrusts'. We shall in due course arrive at an appreciation of their place, but by a sounder method than that in view here.[27]

Another reaction is now proposed. It begins from the belief that, in any Christian judgment, whether in ethical matters or any other, two 'poles' of enquiry or awareness must be held in mind:[28] Christian origins in Jesus as reflected in the New Testament, and the present situation in which the judgment is made. It is not that what lies between in Christian history is of no consequence; rather that, for this purpose, it represents a series of time-conditioned responses and judgments which are parallel to that which we ourselves intend to make.[29] In being on the same footing as ours, as responses made in specific conditions, they do not come to us as a weighty and ever-increasing legacy burdening our shoulders, but as judgments to which ours are peers. They interest and enrich us, but they cannot do our work in our stead. Merely to imitate them is to fail in present responsibility – and in any case illusory, for reproduction of the past in changed circumstances is flawed, bogus parody.

Nor is it the case that Christian origins are normative for us, if by that is meant that they are to dictate our present judgments. The reasons just given for rejecting such use of Christian judgments of the past apply equally to the first Christian responses to Jesus that are to be found in the New Testament. But those first responses, whether ethical or doctrinal in our terms,[30] have a normative character in other ways. There is a practical, down-to-earth sense in which Christian allegiance involves constant and realistic attention to the figure of Jesus, as honest as we can make it, as one of its essential elements, serving as both corrective and guide. That is the religious, as distinct from academic, justification for the historical study of the Gospels and of Jesus as a historical character: to cut away from that point is to lose bearings and identity. There is also a theological sense in which Christian allegiance depends on the belief that the divine is encountered and made known in Jesus – whether that 'making known' is viewed as exclusive or not, and whether 'the divine' is viewed in traditional terms or not.[31] Christian theological, as well as practical, identity is bound up with Jesus, and Christian origins centring on him remain one essential pole in the making of Christian judgments.

But whatever is derived from that source cannot be (and, as

we saw, never truly has been, even in the first decades) determinative. The present also is 'given' to us; and again, in both practical (we have nowhere else to be but the present!) and theological (the living God is the giver) senses. So it is, as one 'present' succeeds another, that Christian judgments differ, even contradict[32] another, with complete legitimacy. We should expect nothing else. The cult of sameness and continuity in Christian moral decisions is misplaced, for new conditions demand and necessitate new responses.

The procedure of taking into account both poles rules out the neglect of either. It rules out, on the one hand, the attempt (vain, as we have seen) merely to imitate the New Testament conditions and decisions, and, on the other hand, sheer conformity to 'the spirit of the age', the colour of the society around us, or of that section of it whose opinions and prejudices we find most to our taste. (This is, of course, much commoner than is ever admitted, as churches merit, all too often, the jibe of being this or that party at prayer.) It means that whatever we now decide must be brought into some contact with the New Testament; equally, that the present must receive the New Testament only when passed through the filter of realistic historical enquiry. That is, attention to the New Testament means letting it 'be' – 'listening to' its voices, and so not making it speak our language, not forcing it to play tunes we like to hear. As far as ever is possible to us, we are to attend to Jesus-via-the New Testament on his terms, not ours, before returning to our situation to make our decisions and judgments, as now required of us.

How, then, is this attention to the New Testament to take place? If the New Testament is not to dictate to us, how are we to make contact with it, how form a grip on it in order to use it? In the light of the cautionary points we have made, it can easily seem elusive, slippery as we seek to grasp it. Let us seek to achieve our aim by considering major features of the making of ethical judgments by Christians in New Testament times. First we list them, looking at them in their own right; then we ask what reflections are aroused, as we return home bearing our discoveries.

1. *New Testament ethics were multiple in inspiration.* Far from being drawn from a single source, such as the teaching of Jesus,[33] the ethical material in the New Testament derives from a wide range of sources. Some of it comes from the surrounding air. It appropriates, sometimes with a minimum of reflection, the current wisdom, both Jewish and Greek. Hence, comparison can be made between Jewish ethics and aspects of the tradition of Jesus' teaching. Paul quotes more or less conventional lists of virtues and vices, patterns of duties for the various members of households, and rules of natural common sense. He can verge on the philosophical by working with the notion of 'the good'.[34]

By contrast, other elements are determined by the patterns of Christ's whole saving work: humility by his embracing of the human lot, generosity by his forsaking the 'riches' of heaven for the 'poverty' of earth.[35] Here, there is a maximum effect of specifically Christian factors on ethics. Or else, there is the taking of Jesus' teaching as a model, which is implicit in its inclusion in the Gospels and in references to it, albeit infrequently, elsewhere.[36] There is also the effect of eschatology – the perspective given to conduct by the short time believed to remain before the End. This undoubtedly conditions many of Paul's ethical judgments, notably his careful counsel for various marital situations in I Corinthians 7.

2. *New Testament ethics are theologically motivated.* Despite the unreflective incorporation of ethical ideas from other extraneous sources, as a whole New Testament ethics are not autonomous, but dependent on theological convictions. Priorities stem from the character of God as now perceived through Jesus and his work. Most strikingly, attention to Jesus' death as the mysterious key to his significance leads to the highlighting of self-denial and humility, on renunciation of the path of power and human approbation, which is either absent from contemporary moral thinking or now given a quite different colouring by its dependence on the career of Jesus.[37]

3. *New Testament ethics differ from writer to writer.* Though various writers have elements in common, it is realistic, from a historical and a theological point of view, to see the teaching of each as having its own validity and as having its place within his thought as a whole. For the individual writer as well as for early Christianity in general, ethics are not a distinct branch of thought but part and parcel of a total theological conception. Even the command to love, reproduced in a wide range of writers, does not have the same connotation for all: various general understandings are reflected in the specific injunctions. Putting it in another way, we can see that each writer has his own moral 'world' in which he lives, his own pressures to respond to, and his own problems to solve.[38]

4. *New Testament ethics are problem-solving in character.* While there is an element in the New Testament of sheer peremptory command in ethical matters,[39] a strong note, especially in a pastoral writing of Paul like I Corinthians, is the attitude of careful attention to the specific details of the matter in hand to the lives of the people addressed.[40] In other words, the tone is not predominantly legislative or judicial, but pastoral. Its aim is more to create good than simply to control evil.

5. *New Testament ethics are concerned with the dilemmas of law and freedom.* Of the issues that occupied the minds of early Christians, none was more prominent than their position in relation to Judaism: was a Christian a kind of Jew, or a new species? If distinct from Jews, how did Christians stand in relation to them — were they their replacement as God's people, their enemies, or their friendly heirs, building on foundations already laid? In this discussion, the Jewish Law was central, and its primary role was in the context of that discussion. Nevertheless, there are elements implicit in the various treatments of the theme of law which relate to deeper and less transient issues: the place of law in human affairs and in relationship with God; the threat of licence when freedom is given, particularly on religious grounds; the degree to which the 'adulthood' of a new relationship with God gives moral maturity and can dispense with the sanctions

and restraints of law. It is evident that some of the churches of the early years found themselves in serious difficulties in relation to these issues.[41]

6 *New Testament ethics as centred on love*. The command to love is the most prominent injunction in the New Testament, occurring in a wide range of writers and in a variety of forms. This predominance is itself related to theological factors: God's love shown in Christ lies deeply at its root, as does its place in the tradition of Jesus' teaching. It points to an ethic which aims at a certain simplicity and is, at least in some conditions, content to leave detailed application in something of an open state.[42]

Each of these features of New Testament ethics has in it much to make the modern Christian ponder. In returning from surveying them to his own day, with ethical problems to face, he cannot fail to be stimulated and enriched. It is not that he returns equipped for immediate decision-making, with his orders in his pocket; but he is changed by the experience he has undergone. We turn to see what lines, in relation to these features, that change might take.

1. *Multiple inspiration*. Christians sometimes feel hesitation or guilt at not offering sufficiently distinctive wisdom to the business of ethical discussion, and at taking on board secular moral thinking, as if it were somehow tainted. They have grown accustomed over the Christian centuries to the exclusive role of society's moral guide, and the loss of that role sometimes stimulates assertiveness to even greater efforts. Yet on many present questions, resulting from wholly new conditions (e.g. in relation to nuclear war, or medical ethics), the Christian tradition is inadequate or non-existent, except at the most general level. The contemplation of New Testament proced-ures may encourage greater self-awareness in this matter and greater willingness to absorb valid moral thinking from any source where it may be found, by putting at least a question-mark against the feelings of hesitation and guilt.

Of all the factors inspiring New Testament ethics, eschato-logy is bound to strike the modern moral thinker as the most dated, the one with least bearing on our situation. Its being obsolete then seems to threaten the impressiveness of much of the ethical teaching which was formed by it. But the eschatological factor itself should not be without resonances for us. It directs our attention towards a certain provisionality in our circumstances, to whose importance we shall return: we judge and decide now as best we can, but the effects of our work and the future lie beyond, in God's hands. There are narrow limits to our importance and to our control. There are purposes beyond our discerning.

2. *The theological motivation of ethics.* Despite their proper openness to all kinds of valid ethical argument, Christians have nevertheless a critique to offer. Its source lies not necessarily in the *content* of the Christian tradition in relation to the matter in hand, but in the basic Christian understanding of God and the priorities of outlook to which it gives rise. That outlook is marked by a sense of the relationship between creator and creature and by the 'general thrusts' (here is their proper place)[43] derived from attention to the figure of Jesus. Even as a matter of sheer identity, a Christian ethic not weighted in these directions is strangely named and seriously exposed to taking on uncritically the colouring of surrounding culture. The Christian critique is then primarily theological, with its ethical outworkings as secondary and always conditioned by the situation in which it takes effect.

3. *Diversity.* I have said quite enough to bring out both the inevitability and the merits of diversity in Christian response. Just as there was no united New Testament ethic, produced by some hidden collusion between the writers, so the New Testament may encourage us to overcome the strong Christian bias, induced over many centuries of natural law theory and of the exercise of ecclesiastical authority, towards uniformity of outlook and universality of moral stance. The variety of settings, in which Christian life so obviously has to be lived throughout the world, now makes such universality a hope which is harder and harder to realize or justify. The New

Testament also encourages the thought that diversity in ethics is not wisely viewed in isolation: ethics relate to theological beliefs, and diversity in the one should be joined to diversity in the other, whether at the level of explicit statement or implicit conviction. Too often, the two live or are made to live separate lives, with sad consequences for both. There is in these considerations, especially as far as world-wide churches are concerned, the material for nothing short of a revolution, with grave repercussions for structures of practice long taken as sacrosanct.

4. *Problem-solving*. Modern Christian ethics, especially in their pastoral application, have been deeply affected by secular movements and their aspirations, notably non-directive counselling with its refusal to make moral judgments and its intent to bring healing and fulfilment to the individual. Much of this is linked without great difficulty to aspects of the Christian tradition and may seem to spring straight from parts of the ministry of Jesus as portrayed in the Gospels. Nevertheless, the legacy of long centuries when a great deal of Christian ethical teaching was affected by legislative and judicial models, backed by the apparatus of church courts and discipline, is not obliterated. In some Christian bodies, it thrives and even finds new expressions, in both great churches and small sects. Both approaches are found in modern Christianity, sometimes in the same churches. They even vie with each other in different aspects of a person's activity: a church leader may assume his official, authoritarian *persona* and then his private, pastoral *persona*, meting out strictures and compassion in alternate hours, in relation to the same moral issue, as he addresses first the public and then an individual in need. There is room for reflection how far the inherited judicial model still has a place. What is the object of Christian moral judgment as exercised by the pastor? Is it a matter of enforcement? or of making moral statements and upholding standards? Or are those aims now remnants of a past when Christianity was, willy-nilly, closely entwined with the judicial and legislative processes of society?

The New Testament may provoke the thought that the priority lies with problem-solving, nourishing the Christian humanity of individuals and groups, not censuring but building up, enabling people to achieve their potential as made in the divine image. In this area as much as any, the New Testament may clear the mind of the Christian decision-maker.

5. *Law and freedom.* The New Testament's 'worry' over this dilemma, conditioned by its time though it is, may induce a certain realism in relation to present tendencies to make easy play with 'freedom' as an unquestionable aspiration, for Christian believers as for everyone. Both the concept and its working out in inner awareness and outward conduct are bedevilled by its role as everybody's slogan. Yet the New Testament's giving of priority to personal relationship (in the first place, with God) over impersonal principle must always find echoes and can always bear reaffirmation.

6. *Love as fundamental.* Study of the treatment of this theme in the New Testament leads to two lines of reflection. First, its connotations then (centring on service, adherence and loyalty) need comparing with those of its use now (centring on warmth, affection and avoidance of all that may cause pain or suggest criticism). Whatever the issue in hand, the comparison is worth making, if only to deter the misuse of New Testament texts. Second, the command to love finds quite distinct senses in the New Testament itself;[44] but despite this variety, its centrality remains. That centrality is worth recalling, as all kinds of other ethical motives press to the surface in our decision-making, whether from within ourselves or from the overwhelmingly technical character of many of the public ethical problems of our day.

Such reflections, given briefly by way of suggestion, inform and enrich us as we return to the present – the second 'pole' involved in our making of ethical judgments. But plainly, the work of making them remains to be done: the New Testament has not done it for us. Moreover, that work, carried out in the light of reflections such as those we have outlined, takes on a character which many find novel and uncongenial. It invites readiness for the following:

1. *Complexity of judgment.* Christian moral theology has a long tradition of subtlety, not to say ingenuity, in arriving at its judgments. Sometimes it is the butt of mockery and complaint on this very score. Yet often, Christians feel pressed into firm, clear decisions on matters of right and wrong which do not readily lend themselves to such treatment. The individual, deciding on some aspect of his own conduct, even feels that clarity ought to be available to him: it can only be his own wilfulness or evasiveness that makes it elude him. The pastor or church spokesman feels pressed by others to make plain statements, and in the background lies a feeling of obligation to the proclamatory strain so prominent in Christian public discourse. Christian statement cannot easily tolerate the hint of indecision. Yet we all know that any moral problem or moral case of any but the utmost simplicity demands the greatest sensitivity to its details and nuances. If we are ever in doubt on that score, we need only turn our attention to problems that concern ourselves: then we discover the rule that moral simplicity is evident chiefly with regard to other people's predicaments.

2. *Revision of judgment.* Change of front comes hard in Christian judgment; yet, rarely admitted, it happens constantly. The myth is that moral, like doctrinal, truth is unchanging.[45] It is better that revision should come, not, as it easily does, from unthinking conformity with transient secular fashion, but from the recognition that a new present demands new judgments. How much Christian discussion of subjects such as war, divorce and homosexual relations has been obfuscated by the failure to see, not only that the witness of scripture (even if unambiguous) cannot end the task for the Christian, but also that changed conditions and genuine advances in knowledge may validly warrant a reversal of judgments made in quite other situations.[46] Faithful response now may even demand a decision directly contrary to that

demanded by faithful response in the past. In reality, the question itself has become a different question.

3. *Provisional solutions.* It follows that no present judgment can necessarily reckon to endure. It represents what the situation now requires, not what it may require in the future. It is desirable that recognition of this factor should not be given reluctantly, but that it should be seen, as our whole discussion has urged, as inherent in the business of Christian decision-making.

4. *Untidy solutions.* Clear thinking may lead, because of the nature of certain cases, to unsatisfactory solutions. In such cases, no neat outcome does justice to all the factors involved, and, with the best will in the world, elements of immorality remain in the course of action prescribed. This situation is well-known in everyday life, and all whose lives and activities are at all complex are accustomed to it. It is commonly dealt with by compartmentalizing activities, so that different moral principles are used in different spheres of life; or else by the adjustment of principle to accommodate the requirements of a problematic area. In either case, conscience is squared. Christian moral teaching sometimes gives the impression of unintentionally conniving at these devices for those who wish to be within its sphere. By its upholding of high or even absolute standards, unintentionally it creates the impression that Christian adherence is for those who can either observe them or become convinced that their departure from them is justifiable. Other people, caught in problematic situations, unable or unwilling to quit them, and reluctant to engage in what they see as hypocrisy, keep away from Christian allegiance, even though on other grounds they may be attracted to it, for example, by believing its doctrinal claims. It is not hard to think of situations in business, political, medical and sexual life where these considerations come into play.

Some of the difficulty arises from the common insistence that Christian moral judgments should be clear-cut and unambiguous – even where life does not easily admit of it. Some springs, however, from sheer error in appropriating Christian wisdom about moral endeavour and its place in relationship with God. Paul's teaching on justification was in no way a licence for moral indifference; but neither was it dependent on the necessary simplicity of moral circumstances, let alone on guarantees of high moral achievement. Rather, by placing God's gracious acceptance first, it gave the setting in which moral endeavour, in thought and practice, could flourish, with forgiveness as its context. In traditional terms, Christianity knows well that penitence is of the essence of the Christian disposition before God, but always in the context of forgiveness and as the basis for moral growth. Yet it often creates the impression that to live in circumstances where such penitence is actually and permanently required is impermissible, lest moral clarity be impaired and genuineness of intent be compromised. In many cases, however the effect is not to discourage indulgence and turpitude but to refuse to countenance situations where conflicting moral demands make neat moral policies impossible. For many people, the acceptance of messy solutions to problems, and recognition that such is their inevitable predicament, is the only possible way in which growth in relationship with God is open to them.

The matter may be put a good deal more positively and less grudgingly. The morally unsatisfactory situation, for example in personal relationship or in priorities in loyalty where family and talent may conflict, is sometimes the necessary condition for creative life. Acceptance of a moral judgment which is untidy but the best available for the time being can be a source of hope and a release of virtue. The New Testament is not without such ambiguities (is it wholly tidy morally to forsake family obligations even for the sake of the kingdom?), and so may contribute directly to the kind of moral awareness which the lines of reflection put forward here may encourage. Like the New Testament they contain a message of moral hope.

-11-

'A Church in Bavaria'

William Plomer, poet, writer and publisher, died in 1973. He is, perhaps, most widely known as the editor of *Kilvert's Diaries*. His autobiography[1] gives little evidence of theological reflection, but in a brief discussion of religious themes, he writes of himself in pre-war days: 'To be deficient in hope is unchristian. I was deficient in hope, and a lapsed Christian.'[2] Yet in his last collection of poems, *Celebrations*, he included 'A Church in Bavaria',[3] which shows a rare understanding of change and variety in Christian faith, as well as of its substance. It teaches a doctrine in which modesty, realism and hope combine. His final stanza encapsulates a world of debate which both theological study and religious commitment are often, to their danger and their loss, reluctant to enter. There is that in even the bravest (or the rashest) of us which finds much in the present state of affairs to press us into inward inconsistency and much that is uncongenial. It is all the same inescapable: we cannot return to former days. Many of its features appear to constitute the direst threat to traditional Christianity. What we need, however, is not reassurance that these things are not truly so, but a framework in which to see them, with both truthfulness and fidelity. So Plomer spoke to our condition.

The poem begins by depicting the interior of a typical Bavarian church, with its riot of decoration:

Everything flows
upward over
chalk-white walls
with the ordered freedom
of a trellised creeper
wreathed and scrolled
in a densely choral
anthem of ornament.

Nimble angels
poise above
in attitudes,
huge-limbed prophets
banner-bearded,
giant apostles,
mitred titans
exemplify
authority.

What Plomer later calls the 'sacred dance' of all these figures reflects a sunny style of Christian piety, assured and unquestioning. Its heart is disclosed in the church's 'focal point':

a seated Virgin,
her covered head
at a fond angle
in accord with
all this swaying
court of images,
looking down
benign and gentle
at the incredible
fact, her Child.

Here, then, is a whole Christian world. Tenderness and consolation are its marks. It is far too complete a culture to know anything of doubt or debate. It has no complaints or difficulties to bring to God. It is a faith imbued with fervent love and a kind of innocence. This church is an Eden restored.

But Christianity is not always like this:

> What does all this
> joyful brilliance
> have to do with
> cults obsessed with
> guilt and sin,
> a punishing angry
> vindictive God?
> Where's that hard
> right-angled object
> the Cross, with Victim
> blanched by torture,
> dead, with blood?

This Christian world answers to human realities and human needs untouched by the paradisal magic of the Bavarian church. And nobody could say that it was inauthentic to deep forces in Christian faith from its outset. Jesus died on Calvary, and Paul found in the cross his glory.

Plomer does not evaluate these two styles of faith, or ask on which side of this apparently impassable chasm we should live. He simply puts them before us. It may be that evaluation is not the poet's business, but the modern theologian may also see sense in his restraint. In the first place we are simply to *know* both.

Both styles remain with us. The baroque church, built perhaps two centuries ago, still stands in Bavaria and helps to form the faith and sensibilities of those who worship in it, though there must be much in their lives to which it is alien. By its nature always an enclave, an Eden apart, now it is much more so. Its architecture, its decoration, its whole 'message' are addressed only obliquely to today. And the same goes for the cross-centred piety as Plomer describes it. Of course it too remains, but not usually in quite the same hyper-realistic form. In that way, both belong strictly to the past – a past in which they once came to birth, as contemporary with a total culture, part and parcel of a world of thought and feeling. They were in every way 'right'. Now, we see things otherwise. The plain concrete church in the next village, devoid of statues and with its plain table-altar, makes the point all too dramatically; and we know that the difference is a matter of theology, not just of economics and building materials.[4]

Yet there is no call for us to make assessment. There is no need to judge those former worlds and test them for adequacy, truth or orthodoxy. We can take them as 'given', elements in a total providence that works with and includes the varied, partial responses of successive groups of believers. We can enter into them, to think and feel with them, then leave them, intact. No response to God has absolute validity; some are grotesque and show no convincing links with that to which they reckon to respond. But all that are expressions of authentic experience resulting from the impact of Jesus have their measure of validity; and we should feel obliged neither to reject them nor to appropriate them. To do either is to assess and judge. We can let them 'be', and we have our own work still to do.

Plomer depicted the two styles of faith. Then he ended his poem with a statement of principle. It is economical in the extreme, but it shows a depth of penetration into our present ills in theological interpretation – less by exposing them than by pointing to a way of receiving our situation with hope and promise. We should dwell upon almost every word.

> Everything bends
>   to re-enact
>   the poem lived,
>   lived, not written,
>   the poem spoken
> by Christ, who never
> wrote a word,
>   saboteur
>   of received ideas

who rebuilt Rome
with the words he
never wrote;
whether sacred,
whether human,
himself a sunrise
of love enlarged,
of love, enlarged.

Everything: it is the fourth occurrence of this word in the poem. In the other cases, its initial reference is to all that is in the church, its total impression. As a whole feature, its effect is to 'say' certain things: 'everything flows upwards' – the pattern of decoration draws the eye from floor to ceiling; 'everything flowers in aspiration' – the riot of ornament represents a burgeoning which draws us to a kind of ecstasy; and 'everything sings in snowy stillness' – the very whiteness of the plaster arouses a lyrical joy, with the purity of a snowy landscape. So the 'everything' refers to the totality of the church, but also speaks more widely of its appeal to us, and so reaches out to include us. Now it goes wider still: *nothing* is excluded from what is now proposed.

bends: the figures in the church wind and turn. Flexibility is a dominant impression of the church and helps to create its softness. It contrasts with 'that hard right-angled object the Cross'. In the same vein, there is the image of a 'trellised creeper'; and there are words like 'flow', 'wreathed', 'scrolled', 'nimble', 'whorls', 'folds', 'corrugations', 'garlands', 'fingering', 'a fond angle'. Of the carved figures of angels, prophets, apostles and bishops, it is said: 'flexible they bend from narrow waists, and raise smooth rounded arms with hands adoring'. But now, 'everything bends'. The decoration of the church reflects reality. There is nothing in life, or in belief, which is rigid, unchanging, not subject to movement and development, not (we may even say) more beautiful for giving itself readily – and being seen to do so – to such readiness to 'bend'. Not just the decoration of the church draws attention to this, but the very fact of its contrast with other, very different styles of Christian piety. Those who built the church may well have seen themselves as witnessing to and representing unchanging faith. They deluded themselves – they were limited and partial in their expression of faith; for 'everything bends'. So commonly resisting this thought, while simultaneously knowing the evidence that shouts it out, Christian theology, and, even more, Christian religious commitment, become brittle if they do not welcome it – 'bend', with grace and with truth.

to re-enact: people fear flexibility because it seems to threaten the destruction of the old and valued. But the words are 'bend' and 're-enact'. What is involved is movement in the old, not the production of mere novelty. So there is genuineness of tradition alongside authenticity of present response; no question of having to choose between slavish adherence to the old and its brusque dismissal. Even intense awareness of discontinuity does not abolish the reality of continuity. We live in traditions, even if their path is tortuous and even as, in certain cases, we denounce them. To take the extreme possibility, even if we go for the antithesis of the old, there may still be a kind of re-enactment.[5]

the poem lived . . . spoken by Christ: it is striking to see a life as a poem. How is that so? A poem is expressive of a vision, and in order to be able to express the vision, never its master. The vision is primary, the well-spring of the poem. To understand the poem, it is necessary to grasp the vision that inspires it. A poem is a construction, yet more than a mere contrivance ('ordered freedom'). There is structure, yet also power. The message may be dogmatic, yet the essence of the act which the poem performs towards us is evocative not authoritarian. It invited us to participate. There is movement and development, perhaps personal immediacy, and yet also an element of inaccessibility and elusiveness, which means that the whole can never be finally grasped or exhausted. So it is with any life. And the more so, the more momentous the life.

A life is not only 'lived', it is also 'spoken' – it is an utterance, directed towards others. This mode of communication, all the more so as the 'speech' is poetic, is subtle, delicate and personal. It is everything that immediately perishes when the mode of discourse changes, for example to the dogmatic or logical or bureaucratic. Christ, like all of us, was no island. In the term used in this book, he, again like us, made his impact on others, diversely, lavishly (and so wastefully), and yet purposefully. He intended to communicate, even though, like all of us, he ran the risk of being falsely or imperfectly understood, all the more so because his mode of communication was speech. A poem lived, a life spoken: the two images intertwine to show the mode and the purpose of Christ's act.

lived not written . . . by Christ, who never wrote a word: perhaps the most fundamental result of historical study of the Gospels, and still one of the most far-reaching, has been the realization of the gap between the life of Jesus and its record. Even when there is no agreement on the width of that gap or how to describe the connection between its two sides, the fact of the gap is acknowledged. When it first dawned, that realization was revolutionary: 'Jesus' could not simply be read off the Gospel page. The 'facts' about Jesus and the 'facts' about the gospel story were not one and the same, nor was the authority of the two. Indeed, the perception of the divergence of the two created a problem, which still presents itself, for those attached to a doctrine of the authority of scripture as ultimate.[6]

An important feature of this discovery is the further recognition that Jesus left no direct written testimony. If the Gospels are not like books dictated on to tape, then we cannot claim to have his voice. He 'never wrote a word'. Everything we have is indirect, responsive to him, the expression of experience to which he gave rise. This is still true even though the Gospels include some of his very words, albeit put from Aramaic into Greek. It is not in the first instance a matter of his words to people, but of various persons' words, as it were, back to him (though couched formally in the manner of address to others, the audiences for whom they were written).

While this is vital for the historian of Christian origins and for the proper appreciation of the Gospels, it is also indispensable for Christian theology and devotion. Speech is the most transient of the modes of human communication, and totally exposed to the risks of loss, misinterpretation, caricature, and adaptation as the memory plays upon it. On this fragile base, the Christian perception of God's self-disclosure deliberately rests; in this fragility, it must be able to find strength and wisdom. These conditions virtually demand the provisional and tentative attitude to theological statement to which modern study points. They also bring home that tentativeness is not weakness: the strength of theological statement lies not in its supposed fixity and durability but in its genuineness as response, as the expression of experience. Moreover, tentativeness means there is space for creativity.

In more dramatic terms, if God chooses to address us thus, must we not be content to reciprocate? If he accepts exposure to such risks, must we not embrace the conditions of discipleship which that implies? It is as if the fluidity of Christian response to God, so clear to the student of Christianity, so strenuously regretted and denied by the organs of authority, was built in from the very start. He never troubled to write a word. (Or, adds the voice of caution, if he did, neither he nor anyone else took trouble to preserve it.)

saboteur: the image suggests both violent and covert activity. Jesus did not simply take Judaism a small step further. In ways not wholly identifiable[7] except in their effects, which may already express fresh turns of ideas and events, he dealt violently with some of its central features. His death was the outcome of that violence: violence meeting violence. Whatever the precise nature and scale of his sabotage, it lit a fuse which led, by a relatively short trail, to the independent existence of the church and Christianity as a 'new' religion. Yet also Jesus worked from within, as it were by stealth. In this way, damage, though real, was somewhat uncertain and mysterious. In a case like this, there is an element of ambiguity worth more attention than Christians have often given it: how 'new' or distinctive is Christianity, originally in relation to Judaism, but also in relation to all other faiths?[8] Is it not worth while to notice the connections as well as the disjunctions, to rebuild rather than always to try to create de novo?

who rebuilt Rome: the effect of Jesus was to destroy 'received ideas', initially in his Jewish environment, ultimately in a wide variety of ways and in all kinds of settings. He is always the potential revolutionary. Though he has been made, abundantly, to play the contrary role of the guarantor of the status quo, for innumerable different régimes and vested interests, his capacity to turn things upside down is always present.

Historically, his sabotage was partly in the sphere of elements of official Judaism, partly in the lives of those who responded to his call. But destruction was not the object of the task: he 'rebuilt' (and we recall the 'ordered freedom' of the church in the opening stanza). What he rebuilt was 'Rome'. The new reality that emerged from Jesus' life was, very soon, wider than the Jewish sphere. It belonged in the broader society of the Roman Empire and thus quickly faced the necessity to adapt to new conditions of thought and institutional life. Immediately, the Gospel was creative and productive; it was mobile, ready to 'bend'. It was also under threat from the very structures that made it possible for it to survive: 'Rome' means exposure to the world.

Judaism itself was not just a religion, and Jesus' own relationship with it illustrates its nature as a social and political reality. 'Rome' emphasizes that aspect of the matter. Jesus gave rise to an entity which was not simply 'spiritual', not simply a new body of 'received ideas', but socio-political. The human needs for peace and justice were within its purview from the start. Its achievements in this area are not alien to the 'poem spoken by Christ' and the sabotage which he carried out, but their direct outcome and valid as their results.

whether sacred, whether human: Plomer's words imply a certain caution and indecisiveness about the person of Christ. How is this elusive, inaccessible, yet potent figure to be described?

181

Christianity has, from the start, had no hesitation in bringing into its response to him that which comes under the heading of the 'sacred'; eventually, the more precise (yet still not clear) term 'divine' becomes appropriate and then dominates. Yet the indecisiveness (as it seems to be from the point of view of the developed tradition) conceals strength; or rather, it raises the question whether this vague way of describing Jesus' status is not wholly sufficient. We need no more, and more may involve a theological wild-goose chase which distracts us from what we really need to see. Jesus was 'of God', and he was certainly flesh of our flesh. Forgetting neither (and so distinguishing ourselves from many of our fellow believers who underplay the one or the other), we can attend to the implications of both. To experience the impact of Jesus is, for the Christian, to enter the sphere of relationship with God and to define its character. It is also to recognize the particularities of Jesus, if not in detail (for we do not know enough of them) then in principle: he was no universal or timeless symbol, but one who had *these* characteristics rather than *those*; not clay on which imagination can work at will, but of specific shape and pattern. It was such a one who was 'of God'.

a sunrise of love enlarged: many and multifarious are the effects which can legitimately be ascribed to the impact of Jesus. They cover, in their ramifications, all kinds of areas of human life and activity. Some are of permanent beauty and marvel, some impenetrable in their opacity to us, some shocking beyond telling. In this book, we have been chiefly concerned with the theological and religious areas; but even there, his effects range widely and sometimes it is hard to discriminate among them. On what principle may we do so? Plomer sees the essence of the freshness of Jesus in the enlarging of love. Though as we saw,[9] love is a shifting commodity, its connotations varying from setting to setting, and not lacking its dangers, it is still better to determine that this should continue to be the effect of Jesus above all else. Plomer put both words to us with deliberation, lest we neglect either the love or the enlargement: 'of love, enlarged'. In that purpose, theology and religion can meet happily.

NOTES

1. Introduction

1. See Yves M. J. Congar, *A History of Theology*, Doubleday, New York, 1968 (originally an article in the *Dictionnaire de Théologie Catholique*; G. R. Evans, *Old Arts and New Theology*, Clarendon Press 1980.

2. See ch. 4 below.

2. The Disintegration of Theology

1. See n. 1, above. Also, Edward Farley, *Theologia: the Fragmentation and Unity of Theological Education*, Fortress Press, Philadelphia 1983.

2. This was the content of the Honour School of Theology at Oxford, established in 1870, and remained so for a hundred years, with minor modifications. It was not dissimilar elsewhere. See Owen Chadwick, *The Victorian Church*, II, A. & C. Black, 1970, pp. 450f.

3. Often, but not always. The most tangled and protracted episode in England surrounded the publication of *Essays and Reviews* in 1860; see Owen Chadwick, op. cit., pp. 75ff.; Ieuan Ellis, *Seven Against Christ*, E. J. Brill 1980.

4. See D. E. Nineham, 'R. H. Lightfoot and the Significance of Biblical Criticism', *Theology* LXXXVIII, Mar. 1985. But there had been numerous earlier instances where 'university' and 'church' interests came into conflict: for the case of E. B. Pusey, see H. C. G. Matthew, 'Edward Bouverie Pusey: From Scholar to Tractarian', *Journal of Theological Studies* XXXII, 1981; for Gore and *Lux Mundi*, 1889, see G. Rowell, *The Vision Glorious*, Oxford University Press 1983, ch. X, and A. M. Ramsey, *From Gore to Temple*, Longmans 1960, chs. I–III; for William Temple, see F. A. Iremonger, *William Temple*, Oxford University Press 1948, ch. VII.

5. E.g. 'Was He Married?', and 'Oh Christianity, Christianity', in Stevie Smith, *Collected Poems*, Allen Lane 1975, pp. 389 and 416.

6. See pp. 43ff below.

7. What is involved here is a sea-change in the possibilities of authority and in attitudes towards it; see D. E. Nineham, *The Use and Abuse of the*

Bible, Macmillan 1976, especially ch. 2; Basil Willey, *The Seventeenth Century Background*, Chatto & Windus 1934, especially ch. 1.

8. The most widely fashionable attempt to achieve a unified theological outlook on the basis of the Bible was the so-called biblical theology movement of the 1940s and 1950s. It has not proved durable. Such attempts are often dogged, even half-consciously, by circumscribed concepts of biblical authority derived from sources extraneous to biblical studies themselves. See J. D. Smart, *The Past, Present and Future of Biblical Theology*, Westminster Press, Philadelphia 1979, and James Barr, *Explorations in Theology 7*, SCM Press, 1980.

3. The Alienation of Theology from Religion

1. See J. Barton, 'Reflections on Cultural Relativism, Parts I & II', *Theology*, LXXXII, 1979; D. E. Nineham, *The Use and Abuse of the Bible*, Macmillan 1976.

2. The point can be grasped by comparing older accounts of the life of Augustine of Hippo, chronicling events and achievements, with Peter Brown's biography (*Augustine of Hippo*, Faber & Faber 1967).

3. For the Trinity in the Old Testament, see, for example, Joseph P. Smith (ed.), *St Irenaeus: Proof of the Apostolic Preaching*, Newman Press New York 1952; and for the development of the doctrine, M. F. Wiles, *The Making of Christian Doctrine*, Cambridge University Press, 1967, especially pp. 124ff.; H. Cunliffe-Jones with Benjamin Drewery (eds.), *A History of Christian Doctrine*, T. & T. Clark and Fortress Press, Philadelphia 1978.

4. See p. 17. For my approach, see J. A. T. Robinson, *The Priority of John*, SCM Press 1985, pp. 365f.

5. For the beginnings of this sense, see Keith Thomas, *Religion and the Decline of Magic*, Weidenfeld & Nicolson 1971, pp. 428f. The OED gives the earliest occurrence of the word with the meaning in view here at 1816.

6. See George Tyrrell, *Christianity at the Cross Roads*, Longmans Green 1910, p. 44.

7. Most plainly in the Gospel of Mark, e.g. 1.22; and the frequent use of 'immediately'.

8. Most clearly in the portrayal of the early Christian missions in the Acts of the Apostles, where the emphasis is on public preaching, a feature not referred to in the letters of Paul.

9. Note the question form in Mark 4.30, inviting shared attentiveness.

10. Compare the ideas of the Gospel as presented in relation to its original context in R. E. Brown, *The Community of the Beloved Disciple*, Geoffrey Chapman 1979, or C. K. Barrett, *The Gospel of John and Judaism*, SPCK 1975, with M. F. Wiles, *The Spiritual Gospel*, Cambridge University

Press 1960, which gives an account of the interpretation of the Gospel of John in the early church.

11. We may point to the re-working of the teaching of Paul to be found in the Letter to the Ephesians and the Pastoral Epistles (see J. L. Houlden, *Paul's Letters from Prison*, Penguin Books 1970, and *The Pastoral Epistles*, Penguin Books 1976), of the thought of the Johannine church of the Gospel in the Johannine Epistles (see R. E. Brown, ibid., and J. L. Houlden, *The Johannine Epistles*, A. & C. Black 1973), and of the thought of Mark in the Gospel of Matthew (see in brief, J. L. Houlden, *Patterns of Faith*, SCM Press 1977, ch. III).

12. See Andrew Louth, *The Origins of the Christian Mystical Tradition*, Clarendon Press 1981; M. F. Wiles and Mark Santer (eds.), *Documents in Early Christian Thought*, Cambridge University Press 1975, ch. 1.

13. See Athanasius, *On the Incarnation*, in E. F. Hardy (ed.), *Christology of the Later Fathers*, Library of Christian Classics, SCM Press and Westminster Press, Philadelphia 1954, especially ch. 54.

14. For its history, see K. E. Kirk, *The Vision of God*, Longmans Green 1931; David Knowles, *The English Mystical Tradition*, Burns & Oates 1961; E. W. Trueman Dicken, *The Crucible of Love*, Darton, Longman & Todd 1963.

15. See the writings of Don Cupitt, especially *Taking Leave of God*, SCM Press 1980.

16. See ch. 9, below. For 'testimony' versus 'evidence' as terms for summing up old and new approaches, see F. E. Crowe, (ed.), *A Third Collection: Papers by Bernard J. F. Lonergan, SJ*, Geoffrey Chapman 1985, p. 80: 'The contrast between pre-critical belief in testimony and critical understanding of evidence is of the greatest theological significance.'

4. Putting Things Together

1. See, for example, R. N. Longenecker, *New Testament Social Ethics for Today*, Eerdmans, Grand Rapids 1984; T. W. Ogletree, *The Use of the Bible in Christian Ethics*, Fortress Press, Philadelphia and Blackwell, 1983; Allen Verhey, *The Great Reversal: Ethics and the New Testament*, Eerdmans, Grand Rapids 1984.

2. See ch. 5, below.

3. See 'Infallibility and Historical Revelation' in Austin Farrer, *Interpretation and Belief* (ed. Charles C. Conti), SPCK 1976.

4. Especially in *Theologia*, Fortress Press, Philadelphia 1983.

5. See Peter Baelz, *An Integrating Theology*, ACCM Occasional Paper 15, London (Church House, Dean's Yard, SW1) 1983.

6. See my 'Liturgy and her Companions', in *Explorations in Theology 3*, SCM Press 1978; and 'Trying to be a New Testament Theologian', in A. E. Harvey (ed.), *Alternative Approaches to New Testament Study*, SPCK 1985.

7. 'Broad thrusts' will reappear in ch. 10, below.

8. See further, p. 169.

9. It is to be noted that some aspects of current New Testament study in fact veer away from the historical perspective, e.g. the application of literary-critical methods, as in F. Kermode, *The Genesis of Secrecy*, Harvard University Press, Cambridge, Mass. 1979, and D. Rhoads and D. Mitchie, *Mark as Story*, Fortress Press, Philadelphia 1982; also the use of structuralist approaches, see B. L. Horne, 'Structuralism, An Introduction', *King's Theological Review* III, 1980, and J. Barr, 'Biblical Language and Exegesis – How Far does Structuralism Help Us?' ibid. VII, 1984. But the great weight of New Testament study is historical in character, an emphasis intensified by the growth of sociological and social-historical work on the text and the earliest churches.

10. And has long been so. For historical perspective on the current dissatisfacton with diversity, see Giles Constable on 'The Diversity of Religious Life and Acceptance of Social Pluralism in the Twelfth Century', in D. Beales and G. Best (eds.), *History, Society and the Churches*, Cambridge University Press 1985, p. 29. The Fourth Lateran Council of 1215 sought to prevent the foundation of new religious orders 'lest the excessive diversity of religious should introduce grave confusion into the church of God'. That which was then opposed was soon to be widely applauded.

11. See further, pp. 64ff.

5. *Starting from the New Testament*

1. We may think of the use made by patristic writers from the mid-second century of the Johannine idea of Jesus as the 'Word' (Logos), transmuting it into a much more philosophical idiom; or of the taking of the idea of Jesus' pre-existence, found in at most three New Testament writers, and the making of it by Origen in the early third century a central focus for the understanding of Jesus. (See, for example, relevant sections of J. N. D. Kelly, *Early Christian Doctrines*, A. & C Black, 1958.)

2. In this cause, see the notable work of E. P. Sanders in *Paul and Palestinian Judaism*, SCM Press and Fortress Press, Philadelphia 1977, and *Paul, the Law, and the Jewish People*, Fortress Press 1983 and SCM Press 1985; and K. Stendahl, *Paul among Jews and Gentiles*, Fortress Press and SCM Press 1977.

3. There have been times and places where Christians have appreciated diversity, though not always for liberal-minded reasons; see Giles Constable, art cit. (n. 9 above), p. 46 and his n. 65.

4. See further, ch. 7 below.

5. On the political involvement view, see E. Bammel and C. F. D. Moule (eds.), *Jesus and the Politics of His Day*, Cambridge University Press 1984. Others: G. Vermes, *Jesus and the World of Judaism*, SCM Press and Fortress Press, Philadelphia 1983; A. E. Harvey, *Jesus and the Constraints of*

History, Duckworth 1982; E. P. Sanders, *Jesus and Judaism*, SCM Press and Fortress Press 1985.

6. By no means all of the writers mentioned in n. 5 underplay Jesus' distinctiveness within the setting of his day, notably Harvey and Sanders.

7. I found this expression particularly helpful in *Patterns of Faith*, SCM Press 1977, pp. 66ff.

8. See J. Knox, *The Death of Christ*, Collins 1958, ch. 7.

9. The following passages may be referred to alongside the points that have just been made: Col. 2.15; Rom. 8. 35–39; II Cor. 3; Gal. 3; Rom. 5.12ff.; I Cor. 1:24; II Cor. 5.17–19.

10. See the works of E. P. Sanders referred to in n. 2 above; also H. Räisänen, *Paul and the Law*, J. C. B. Mohr, Tübingen 1983.

11. See ch. 11 below. Also Werner H. Kelber, *The Oral and the Written Gospel*, Fortress Press, Philadelphia 1983.

12. As Paul found, I Cor. 14.

13. See I Cor. 12–14, especially ch. 14. See Bengt Holmberg, *Paul and Power*, C. W. K. Gleerup, Lund 1978; R. Banks, *Paul's Idea of Community*, Paternoster Press 1980, especially ch. 10.

14. Most clearly shown in II Peter 3.15f. and the Letter of James; but Ephesians and the Pastoral Epistles (I and II Timothy and Titus) show writers imitating and using Paul but adapting his words and ideas to their own different purposes.

15. See n. 14, above; also note the interrelationships of the Synoptic Gospels.

16. I Cor. 15.8.

17. I Cor. 15.3ff. is generally thought to be an early summary of belief, and Phil. 2.6–11 an early hymn about Christ.

18. The clearest examples from early Christianity are the decisions, especially creeds and similar formulas, of formal councils. See J. N. D. Kelly, *Early Christian Creeds*, Longmans 1950, and Hans von Campenhausen, *Ecclesiastical Authority and Spiritual Power*, A. & C. Black 1969.

19. For early examples, see the process leading up to the councils of Nicaea and Chalcedon. Cf. H. Chadwick, *The Early Church*, Penguin Books, Fortress Press, 1967; W. H. C. Frend, *The Rise of Christianity*, Fortress Press, Philadelphia and Darton, Longman & Todd 1984.

20. For random examples of this distinction operating in popular manifestations of Christianity, see P. Brown, *The Cult of the Saints*, SCM Press 1981; E. Le Roy Ladurie, *Montaillou*, Scolar Press 1978; G. J. Cuming & Derek Baker (eds.), *Popular Belief and Practice*, Cambridge University Press 1972.

21. What is in mind here are factors like the decline in teaching by rote and so absorbing of a stock of forms of words like collects, psalms, and hymns; the movement away from familiarity with a single version of the Bible; the loss of a traditional and euphonious liturgy, with its memorable phrases and formulas.

22. E.g. in the former pervasiveness in English culture of the Book of Common Prayer and the Authorized Version of the Bible.

23. It is churches themselves that have been instrumental in producing new liturgies, encouraging new styles of worship, sponsoring new translations of the Bible, and generally introducing variety and informality in the verbal expressions of belief which believers find at their disposal.

24. Modern examples are church reports on moral and social issues, and the fruits of ecumenical negotiations. Whatever wider standing they may achieve (e.g. acceptance by churches as official bodies), these bear the marks of the groups which produce them and result from give and take in the work which has led to them.

25. See the works listed in n. 2 above.

26. This element is of course not absent from Paul, cf. Gal. 2.20; Phil. 3.8ff. What is in mind here is overall impression, and the words 'edges towards' are important.

27. See *English Hymnal* 419 and 115.

28. See (e.g.) K. F. Nickle, *The Synoptic Gospels*, SCM Press and John Knox Press, Atlanta 1982; R. P. Martin, *New Testament Foundations, The Four Gospels*, Paternoster Press 1975.

29. Particularly instructive for understanding this approach are: D. Rhoads and D. Michie, *Mark as Story*, Fortress Press, Philadelphia 1982, and E. Best, *Mark: the Gospel as Story*, T. & T. Clark 1983.

30. The two elements are well combined in Athanasius' *On the Incarnation* (in E. R. Hardy and C. C. Richardson (eds.), *Christology of the Later Fathers*, Library of Christian Classics, SCM Press, and Westminster Press, Philadelphia 1954), written probably just a few years after the end of the Great Persecution and Constantine's Peace of the Church.

31. The development of this approach owes a great deal, at the fundamental level, to the work of Peter Berger, in whose books the vocabulary used below is expounded. See especially (with Thomas Luckmann) *The Social Construction of Reality*, Penguin Books 1967; *A Rumour of Angels*, Penguin Books 1970; *The Social Reality of Religion*, Penguin Books 1973, first published in the USA in 1967 under the title *The Sacred Canopy*.

32. See p. 117.

33. For rejection, see Marcion (H. Chadwick, *The Early Church*, Penguin Books 1967, pp. 38–40; R. Joseph Hoffmann, *Marcion: On the Restitution of Christianity*, Scholars Press, Chico, California 1984), and for the nearest to pure continuity, see the Ebionites, obscure as they are (J. N. D. Kelly, *Early Christian Doctrines*, A. & C. Black 1958, pp. 139f.).

34. See e.g. Matt. 16.28; 26.64; I Cor. 15. 20–28; Rev. 22.20.

6. The New Testament and the Religious Quest

1. See Robert L. Wilken, *The Myth of Christian Beginnings*, SCM Press 1979. From the earliest period, we may note the use – and adaptation –

of Pauline teaching by the writers of Ephesians and the Pastoral Epistles; and from later times, the viewing of Paul through what we now see as distorting spectacles by Augustine in the late fourth and early fifth centuries and by Luther in the sixteenth. (See K. Stendahl, *Paul among Jews and Gentiles*, Fortress Press, Philadelphia and SCM Press 1977.)

2. This has happened not only among determinedly conservative theologians but also, in effect, in the biblical theology movement of the 1940s and 1950s and, in another way, in the liturgical movement of the past half-century.

3. Cf. p. 12.

4. There is an interesting account of the rise and fall of this mode of religious discourse in G. Steiner, *On Difficulty and Other Essays*, Oxford University Press 1978, especially pp. 82ff.

5. In various ways, such an approach is encouraged by such works as Northrop Frye, *The Great Code*, Routledge & Kegan Paul 1982; Paul Ricoeur, *Essays on Biblical Interpretation*, SPCK 1981; and structuralist interpretations of the biblical text.

6. For the debate on this issue, see W. J. Abraham, *Divine Revelation and the Limits of Historical Criticism*, Oxford Univesity Press 1982; James Barr, *The Bible in the Modern World*, SCM Press 1973; and *Explorations in Theology* 7, SCM Press, 1980.

7. See E. D. Hirsch, Jr, *The Aims of Interpretation*, University of Chicago Press 1976, especially pp. 1–13, 79–81; and Peter Ackroyd, *T. S. Eliot*, Hamish Hamilton 1984, p. 120.

8. See my 'Liturgy and her Companions', in *Explorations in Theology* 3, SCM Press 1978.

9. See ch. 9, below.

10. E.g. Mark 1.22.

11. For Acts, see E. Haenchen, *The Acts of the Apostles*, Blackwell and Westminster Press, Philadelphia, 1971; and for Paul, see R. F. Hock, *The Social Context of Paul's Ministry*, Fortress Press, Philadelphia 1980; Wayne A. Meeks, *The First Urban Christians*, Yale Univerity Press 1983; and I Corinthians.

12. See also ch. 10 below.

7. Being in a Tradition

1. On Gore and *Lux Mundi*, see A. M. Ramsey, *From Gore to Temple*, Longmans 1960; G. Rowell, *The Vision Glorious*, Oxford University Press 1983, ch. X; J. Carpenter, *Gore: a Study in Liberal Catholic Thought*, Faith Press 1960.

2. On Henson, see Owen Chadwick, *Hensley Henson*, Clarendon Press 1983, p. 105 and ch. 6.

3. A. M. Ramsey, op. cit. (n. 1 above), pp. 100ff., 109f.

4. Alec Vidler (ed.), *Soundings*, Cambridge University Press 1962; cf. review by H. Chadwick in *Theology* LXV, 1962, pp. 441ff.

5. A. M. Ramsey, op. cit., pp. 109f.

6. Stephen Platten, 'The Attractiveness of Radical Catholicism', *Theology* LXXXV, 1982, pp. 429ff.

7. Shakespeare, *Twelfth Night*, Act 1, Scene 5.

5. J. O. Johnston, *Life and Letters of Henry Parry Liddon*, 1904, p. 365, quoted in G. Rowell, op. cit., pp. 221f.

9. See I Cor. 15.3ff.

10. See R. P. C. Hanson, *Tradition in the Early Church*, SCM Press 1962.

11. See, for example, Owen Chadwick, *From Bossuet to Newman*, Cambridge University Press 1957; R. L. Wilken, *The Myth of Christian Beginnings*, SCM Press 1971.

12. See R. A. Markus, *Christianity in the Roman World*, Thames & Hudson 1974, pp. 51–61.

13. See H. Chadwick, *The Early Church*, Penguin Books 1967, pp. 38–40; R. J. Hoffmann, *Marcion: on the Restitution of Christianity*, Scholars Press, Chico, California 1984.

14. See my *Ethics and the New Testament*, Mowbray 1973, ch. 2; *Patterns of Faith*, SCM Press 1977, ch. 3.

15. See n. 11, above; also review of D. L. Edwards, *Christian England*, Vol. II, by J. S. Morrill, in *Theology* LXXXVII, 1984, pp. 212ff., referring to 'pervasive disrespect for the integrity of the past', when history is viewed in relation to its contribution to the present.

16. Early third-century author of *The Apostolic Tradition*, ed. Gregory Dix, SPCK 1937, containing a Roman eucharistic liturgy in ch. iv. See also C. P. M. Jones, G. Wainwright, and E. Yarnold, *The Study of Liturgy*, SPCK 1978.

17. Compare John 1.1 with I John 1.1; 2.7, 24, and see my *The Johannine Epistles*, A. & C. Black 1973, pp. 15, 48f.

18. J. H. Newman, *Difficulties of Anglicans*, II, 1891, pp. 80f.; see Peter Brown, *Society and the Holy in Late Antiquity*, Faber & Faber, 1982, 'Learning and Imagination', p. 11.

19. See David Knowles, *The Historian and Character*, Cambridge University Press 1963, ch. 12; Adrian Morey, *David Knowles: A Memoir*, Darton, Longman & Todd 1979.

20. See especially Romans 9–11.

21. See ch. 11, below. An earlier version of this essay was given as a paper to the Bristol Theological Society.

8. What to Believe about Jesus

1. It is possible that the christological statement in Col. 1.15–20 is included partly for controversial purposes, less likely that it was composed with such purposes in view. Hebrews 1, insisting that Christ is

'the Son' and no mere angel, is another candidate for consideration, but it is scarcely a matter of doctrinal quandary in the later sense.

2. *The Myth of God Incarnate*, ed. J. Hick, SCM Press 1977.

3. A term coined by M. D. Goulder for those who contributed to *The Myth of God Incarnate*.

4. *Incarnation and Myth*, ed. M. D. Goulder, SCM Press 1979.

5. *God Incarnate, Story and Belief*, ed. Anthony Harvey, SPCK 1981.

6. C. E. Gunton, *Yesterday and Today*, Darton, Longman & Todd 1983.

7. Graham Shaw, *The Cost of Authority*, SCM Press 1983, p. 274.

8. E.g. A. E. Harvey (n. 5 above); James P. Mackey, *Jesus, the Man and the Myth*, SCM Press 1979; E. Schillebeeckx, *Jesus*, Collins 1979, and *Christ*, SCM Press 1980.

9. Notably in Parts 1 and 4 of *Christ*.

10. I.e. on Father, Son, and Spirit. The same point was raised by G. W. H. Lampe in *God as Spirit*, Clarendon Press 1977.

11. *Essays on John*, SPCK 1982, pp. 33f. Cf. also my own 'The Place of Jesus' in M. D. Hooker and C. Hickling (eds.), *What about the New Testament?*, SCM Press 1975.

12. See the influential R. Bultmann, *Jesus Christ and Mythology*, SCM Press 1960; and *The Myth of God Incarnate*.

13. See my 'The Doctrine of the Trinity and the Person of Christ', in *Explorations in Theology* 3, SCM Press 1978.

14. On the status of New Testament titles for Jesus, see M. D. Hooker, *The Message of Mark*, Epworth Press 1983, pp. 64ff.

15. See J. D. G. Dunn, *Christology in the Making*, SCM Press 1980.

16. See essays by Frances Young and M. D. Goulder in Part One of *The Myth of God Incarnate*, pp. 13–121.

17. See ch. 3 above.

18. Indeed in the recent past: see C. F. D. Moule, *The Origin of Christology*, Cambridge University Press 1977; and J. D. G. Dunn, op. cit. (n. 15 above).

19. See John 1.1–3, 14 (creator-word); 1.17 (law); 2.21 (templc); 19.36 (Passover).

20. See M. F. Wiles, *The Spiritual Gospel*, Cambridge University Press 1960; T. E. Pollard, *Johannine Christology and the Early Church*, Cambridge University Press 1970.

21. See the idea of the intertwining of 'stories', pp. 83ff. above.

22. For an assault on fantasy in the name of history, see E. P. Sanders, *Jesus and Judaism*, SCM Press 1985.

23. See above, pp. 83ff.

24. An earlier version of this essay was given as a paper to the Hort Theological Society, Cambridge.

9. The Resurrection

1. E.g. C. F. Evans, *Resurrection and the New Testament*, SCM Press 1970; Willi Marxsen, *The Resurrection of Jesus of Nazareth*, SCM Press 1970; R. H. Fuller, *The Formation of the Resurrection Narratives*, SPCK 1972; Don Cupitt, *Explorations in Theology* 6, SCM Press, 1979, ch. 4 (correspondence with C. F. D. Moule). For an interesting treatment of stories not in the Gospels and for possible effects of OT passages, see J. D. Crossan, *Four Other Gospels*, Winston Press, Minneapolis, 1985.

2. In many statements, crises, and controversies of the last hundred years, the two have figured together as the two great 'gospel miracles': e.g. James Carpenter, *Gore*, Faith Press 1960, pp. 106f.; F. A. Iremonger, *William Temple*, Oxford University Press 1948, ch. vii, Owen Chadwick, *Hensley Henson*, Clarendon Press 1983, ch. 6, p. 135.

3. See R. E. Brown, *The Birth of the Messiah*, Geoffrey Chapman 1977, especially Appendix IV; H. von Campenhausen, *The Virgin Birth in the Theology of the Ancient Church*, SCM Press 1964.

4. See p. 185n.16, above.

5. See Don Cupitt, *Christ and the Hiddenness of God*, Lutterworth Press 1971 reissued SCM Press 1985, ch. 9, pp. 141f.; L. Festinger, *When Prophecy Fails*, Harper & Row, New York 1964.

6. See C. F. Evans, op. cit., ch. I.

7. See I Cor. 7.31; 10.11; Rom. 6.3ff.

8. The verb *hupsoō* (= exalt, lift up) is used with reference to Christ's mode of death, in a kind of theological pun: John 3.14; 8.28; 12.32. For 'glory', see, e.g., John 13.31f; 17.1, 4f.

9. See John 20–21.

10. There are elements in the Fourth Gospel which reserve something for a final resurrection of the dead (5.25–29; 6.39f., 44), and there is dispute whether these are intrusive into the dominant view of the Gospel, possibly the result of a stage in the Gospel's composition when more conventional doctrine was felt to need a witness. For a reaction to an extreme version of the 'resurrection now' view, see II Tim. 2.18.

11. See his *On the Incarnation* (cf. ch. 5 n. 30), chs. 20–32.

12. See (e.g.) Gregory of Nyssa, *Address on Religious Instruction*, ch. 37 (in Hardy and Richardson, op. cit., ch. 5 n. 30).

13. Athanasius, op. cit., chs. 30, 46.

14. The Fathers would not have been amused by the Yorkshire song, 'On Ilkley Moor'.

15. H. A. Williams, *True Resurrection*, Mitchell Beazley 1972; Peter Berger sees moves in the direction taken by Williams as a natural concomitant of the subjectifying of religion in a secularized society (see *The Social Reality of Religion*, Penguin Books 1967, p. 168).

16. See above, pp. 62ff. Also my *Patterns of Faith*, SCM Press 1977, pp. 66–82.

17. A tendency which may be discerned in the transition from the Gospel of Mark, which concentrates on Jesus' death in its own right, to that of Luke, where there is a sense of its being 'put right' by the resurrection and ascension which follow and which figure so prominently.

18. Because the risen Christ (as distinct from the earthly Jesus) *can* be seen as having few characteristics apart from power and splendour, he is all too easily made the guarantor and sponsor of earthly grandeur and power in Christian institutions and individuals. Jesus then becomes the fount of characteristics the opposite of those to which the Gospels testify. The tendency goes back at least as far as Eusebius in the early fourth century. For him, Jesus is the super-emperor; and in his *Ecclesiastical History*, he actually ignores the story of Jesus' death!

19. See L. Boros, *The Moment of Truth*, Burns & Oates 1962.

20. See also Hab. 3. 17f.; Gal. 6.14; the well-known hymns 'My God, I love thee' and 'Lord, it belongs not to my care' (*English Hymnal* 80 and 433).

21. See Romans 8.35–39.

22. The strength of Farrer's emphasis on this point is well brought out in Philip Curtis's biography, *A Hawk among Sparrows*, SPCK 1985, ch. 12. It must be said that Farrer failed to make a perfect join on this matter betwee his faithfulness to traditional doctrine and historical considerations. Indeed, by 'the resurrection of the dead', to which he constantly appealed, he seemed to mean immortality as life with God as a perfecting and judging gift – as in his sermon, 'The Ultimate Hope' (*A Celebration of Faith*, Hodder & Stoughton 1970, pp. 117ff.). He showed marvellously the congruity of the resurrection with many other convictions, but here more than anywhere in his thought faith became just that, and assertion replaced real argument. For him as for us, the issue resolves itself into the possibility of detaching 'resurrection' from its Jewish apocalyptic setting, a move which modern historical consciousness finds increasingly uncongenial. (See also A. M. Farrer, *Saving Belief*, Hodder and Stoughton, 1964.)

10. Ethical Decisions and the New Testament

1. Anyone interested in the more exegetical aspect of this subject may read this essay as a continuation into the area of application of the work presented in my *Ethics and the New Testament*, Mowbray 1973.

2. From the divorce proceedings of Henry VIII (see J. J. Scarisbrick, *Henry VIII*, Eyre & Spottiswoode 1968, ch. VII) to church reports of recent times such as *Homosexual Relationships* (Church Information Office 1979; see also my 'How Far Will the Past Take Us? Bible, Tradition and Homosexual Relationships', *Crucible*, July-September 1980, and Robin Scroggs, *The New Testament and Homosexuality*, Fortress Press, Philadelphia 1983).

3. For the earliest instance of something like a systematic consideration see Ptolemaeus' *Letter to Flora* from the first half of the second century (ed. R. McL. Wilson, *Gnosis*, by Werner Foerster, Clarendon Press, 1972, pp. 154ff.).

4. See, for example, the precedence given, from a Christian standpoint, to the prophetic writings rather than the Law, as Judaism would perceive the matter, in C. H. Dodd, *The Authority of the Bible*, Collins Fontana 1960 (originally published 1929).

5. For classical versions, see, for example, Paul Althaus, *The Theology of Martin Luther*, Fortress Press, Philadelphia 1966, ch. 9; F. Wendel, *Calvin*, Collins Fontana 1963, ch. 3. For a recent essay see E. W. Kemp (ed.), *Man, Fallen and Free*, Hodder & Stoughton 1969, essays by J. A. Baker and J. L. Houlden.

6. Consider, for example, the following passages: Matt. 5.17–20; I Cor. 9.8ff.; I Cor. 10.1–13; Rom. 13.8–10.

7. See n. 2, above.

8. For practical discussion of the use of the Bible in a specific matter, see, for example, *Marriage, Divorce, and the Church* (The Root Report), SPCK 1971.

9. See my *Ethics and the New Testament*, ch. 3i.

10. See Martin Hengel, *Property and Riches in the Early Church*, SCM Press and Fortress Press, Philadelphia 1974; David L. Mealand, *Poverty and Expectation in the Gospels*, SPCK 1980; L. W. Countryman, *The Rich Christian in the Church of the Early Empire*, Edwin Mellen Press, New York 1980.

11. Mark 10.17–31.

12. See Robert Banks, *Paul's Idea of Community*, Paternoster Press 1980; Gerd Theissen, *The Social Setting of Pauline Christianity*, Fortress Press, Philadelphia and T. & T. Clark 1982; Wayne A. Meeks, *The First Urban Christians*, Yale University Press 1983.

13. E.g. 4.18ff; 6.20; 16.19–31.

14. 'The Rich Man's Salvation', translated by G. W. Butterworth, Loeb Classical Library, Heinemann 1919.

15. Mark 1.16–20; 10.28ff.; Matt. 8.21f.; Luke 14.26.

16. John 9; see J. L. Martyn, *History and Theology in the Fourth Gospel*, Harper & Row, New York 1968; R. E. Brown, *The Community of the Beloved Disciple*, Geoffrey Chapman 1979.

17. Col. 3.18ff.; Eph. 5.22ff.; II Tim. 1.5.

18. For attempts to reach compromise positions, see the works listed in ch. 4, n. 1.

19. See above, p. 98.

20. See R. E. Brown, op. cit., pp. 123ff.; J. L. Houlden, *Ethics*, pp. 35ff.; Jack T. Sanders, *Ethics in the New Testament*, Fortress Press Philadelphia, and SCM Press 1975, ch. V.

21. I John 2.5; 4.7–12 in the light of 2.18ff.; 4.1–6. Compare I John 3.16f. with II John 10f.

22. See, for example, the works listed in ch. 4, n. 1.

23. Consider, for example, the status of scripture as referred to in a debate of the General Synod of the Church of England on experimentation on embryos (*Report of Proceedings*, February 1985, Vol. 16, no. 1, Church Information Office 1985). An examination candidate once offered as the key text for the making of Christian judgments in connection with labour relations today, 'Slaves, be obedient to those who are your earthly masters' (Eph. 6.5).

24. Perhaps most strikingly in I Cor. 7; see especially vv. 29–31.

25. Christians differ, in ways often related to social group, political affiliation, and education, on matters such as capital punishment, nuclear disarmament, and attitudes to oppressive régimes.

26. See Allen Verhey, *The Great Reversal*, Eerdmans, Grand Rapids 1984, ch. IV.

27. See p. 167 below.

28. See Schillebeeckx, *Christ*.

29. Or, to use the image used elsewhere in the same circle with us.

30. For the New Testament itself makes no such neat categorization.

31. See ch. 8 above.

32. Anyone doubting the capacity of Christians to contradict previous judgments without noticing it may consider the giving of permission in 1985 to Roman Catholics in England and Wales to receive communion in both kinds. A spokesman, asked about the danger of chalices being spilt, said, 'If there is a spillage you quietly mop it up.' There could be no clearer sign that traditional and official doctrine about the eucharist is no longer believed, for genuine belief in transubstantiation would make such a reaction as impossible now as it has been in the past. The moral is that beliefs change unnoticed and unadmitted. The present papal espousal of human rights is also a matter of interest when put alongside the *Syllabus Errorum* issued by Pius IX in 1864. See Austin Farrer's 'Infallibility and Historical Revelation', in *Interpretation and Belief*, SPCK 1976.

33. Pre-critical use of the New Testament drew no distinction between what Jesus taught and what the Gospels record him as teaching.

34. See Rom. 1.29–31; Col. 3.18–4.1; I Cor. 11.14; Rom. 12.9, 21: one example of each category referred to in the text.

35. See Phil. 2.1–11 and II Cor. 8.9.

36. I Cor. 7.10; 9.14; Acts 20.35.

37. II Cor. 12.9f.; Phil. 1.21; Gal. 6.14.

38. See works referred to in nn. 1, 18, and 20 above.

39. See, for example, I Cor. 16.22; and E. Käsemann, 'Sentences of Holy Law in the New Testament', in *New Testament Questions of Today*, SCM Press and Fortress Press 1969.

40. See John C. Hurd, *The Origin of I Corinthians*, SPCK 1965; John W. Drane, *Paul, Libertine or Legalist?*, SPCK 1975.

41. It is one aspect of issues dealt with in, for example, I Cor. 8; 10; 11.

See also Paul's sarcasm in a passage like I Cor. 4.8. This is an area where anachronistic judgments have been made more often than almost anywhere. Modern-style issues of freedom are not as directly present as is often assumed: see E. P. Sanders, *Paul, the Law, and the Jewish People*, Fortress Press, Philadelphia 1983 and SCM Press 1985. But for a positive statement of the continuing force of Paul's analysis, in Galatians in particular, see C. K. Barrett, *Freedom and Obligation*, SPCK 1985.

42. See V. P. Furnish, *The Love Command in the New Testament*, Abingdon Press and SCM Press 1973.

43. See n. 42 above.

44. Restricted to the neighbour in Mark 12.31; Rom. 13.9; extended to enemies in Matt. 5.14; confined to the community of believers in John 13.34.

45. See n. 32 above.

46. See nn. 2 and 8 above.

11. 'A Church in Bavaria'

1. *The Autobiography of William Plomer*, Jonathan Cape 1975.

2. Ibid. p. 317.

3. Now in *Collected Poems*, Jonathan Cape 1973, pp. 256ff.

4. See ch. 10 n. 32 above.

5. See ch. 7 above.

6. For is not the authority of Jesus 'more ultimate' than that of scripture?

7. For a recent and candid attempt to identify them, see E. P. Sanders, *Jesus and Judaism*, SCM Press, 1985.

8. See Alan Race, *Christians and Religious Pluralism*, SCM Press and Orbis Books, Mary Knoll 1983; Paul F. Knitter, *No Other Name?*, Orbis Books and SCM Press 1985.

9. See above, p. 169.

INDEX